P9-EEJ-748

SENSATIONAL TRIALS

OF THE 20TH CENTURY

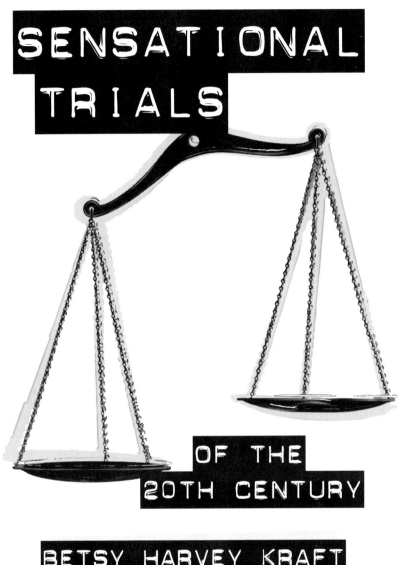

BETSY HARVEY KRAFT

SCHOLASTIC PRESS · NEW YORK

ACKNOWLEDGMENTS

I am indebted to those who provided support during the writing of this book. Special thanks go to Roger Adelman for generously sharing his knowledge of the law; Carrie Bruns for her guidance in photo research; Sheila Blake for her thoughtful review; and Scholastic Press editor Ann Reit for her professional encouragement.

Copyright © 1998 by Betsy Harvey Kraft

All rights reserved. Published by Scholastic Press, a division of Scholastic Inc., *Publishers since 1920*. SCHOLASTIC and SCHOLASTIC PRESS and associated logos are trademarks and/or registered trademarks of Scholastic Inc.

No part of this publication may be reproduced, or stored in a retrieval system, or transmitted in any form or by any means, electronic, mechanical, photocopying, recording, or otherwise, without written permission of the publisher. For information regarding permission, write to Scholastic Inc., Attention: Permissions Department, 555 Broadway, New York, NY 10012.

Library of Congress Cataloging-in-Publication Data

Kraft, Betsy Harvey
Sensational trials of the twentieth century / Betsy Harvey Kraft.
p.   cm.
Includes index.
Summary: Presents accounts of eight significant trials in the twentieth century, including the Scopes trial, Watergate, *Brown* v. *Board of Education*, and the Hinckley trial.

ISBN 0-590-37205-X

1. Trials—United States—Juvenile literature. [1. Trials] 1. Title
KF220.K73   1998   347.73'7 — dc21
97-49432   CIP   AC

10 9 8 7 6 5 4 3 2 1   8 9/9 0/0 01 02 03

Printed in the U.S.A.   37
First edition, November 1998
Design by David Caplan

For Michael Baker Kraft, a seeker of justice

CONTENTS

INTRODUCTION

Americans love trials. For more than one hundred years they have crowded into courtrooms, read newspapers, listened to radios, and sat before television screens — just to feel a part of the real-life dramas unfolding before them.

Every day there are trials all over the United States. Most of them go unnoticed. Some, however, become sensations. Throughout the twentieth century many lawyers thought *their* trial was the "trial of the century." At the time, of course, it was. But before long a new trial would come along to replace the old, a new trial with new personalities and new issues. And that one would become the *new* "trial of the century."

When a trial does become a sensation, hundreds, sometimes thousands, of people show up for it. Celebrities arrive, providing glitter and excitement. Lawyers become famous. Witnesses, once unknown, become household names. Seedy characters obsessed with trial-watching hang around the hallways of court buildings, offering opinions. Jurors, ordinary people from all walks of life, are asked to make extraordinary judgments. Reporters scramble for stories and photographers jostle for the best pictures. At the center of the circus, judges try to maintain order and strive to be fair.

For the accused and the plaintiff, the spectacle is often brutal. There are few secrets in courtrooms. The most personal aspects of their lives become public. Gossip and rumors abound, and truths are revealed. Families break up, fortunes are made and lost, and reputations are destroyed. Meanwhile, America looks on with fascination.

Trials are more than entertainment, though. They are part of America's history as well as its future. What happens in court reflects the beliefs of the people. Decisions made by juries and judges often change the way we live. Through trials Americans confront some of their most important concerns, concerns like immigration, religion, crime, and individual rights. Trials force people to think about their political system, the treatment of the mentally ill, and racial issues.

Important trials almost always bring change. New laws are passed and new customs and beliefs replace old, outdated ones. Sometimes trials bring justice. Certainly that is what people expect. But mistakes are sometimes made. Verdicts are sometimes wrong, and they are often unpopular. And what one jury thinks is just may not be what another jury would think. But the search for justice goes on. And America's search for the "trial of the century" continues.

"A GOOD SHOEMAKER AND A POOR FISH PEDDLER"

THE SACCO-VANZETTI TRIAL

The holiday season was a busy time for Bartolomeo Vanzetti, an Italian fish peddler selling eels and codfish from a cart on the streets of Plymouth, Massachusetts. He was there, the immigrant said later, early on the morning of December 24, 1919, delivering fish for the holidays. According to Vanzetti, he had been up before dawn and had gone into a neighborhood bakery shop at 7:45 that morning. His thirteen-year-old helper said he had been with Vanzetti just before eight o'clock. The exact times were important. Vanzetti said he was peddling fish, but the police disagreed. They said he was committing armed robbery.

That morning, twenty-eight miles from Plymouth in the quiet town of Bridgewater, an armored truck headed up Broad Street. It carried two security guards and $30,000 in cash, money for Christmas paychecks for the workers at the White Shoe Company. Suddenly the truck was blocked by a large dark Buick. Two men, one with a shotgun, the other with a revolver, leapt out and opened fire on the security guards. With the truck still moving, one of the guards drew his gun and shot wildly from the windows. Careening crazily on the icy street, the driver lost control of the truck and crashed into a telephone pole. Within seconds the gunmen jumped back into their getaway car, leaving the guards shaken but unharmed. The time was 7:45 A.M. The gunmen, a witness said, did not look familiar. They looked "dark," and "not American."

Four months after the Christmas Eve holdup failed, a second, more deadly crime occurred. Again, it involved a payroll robbery, this one in nearby South Braintree. Again, the police thought Vanzetti was one of the gunmen. At three o'clock on the afternoon of April 15, 1920, a company paymaster and a guard carrying a .38 revolver stacked fifteen thousand dollars in cash into two metal boxes. Then they began the short walk from the company offices to the factory. About halfway down Pearl Street, two men in dark clothes and caps stepped onto the sidewalk in front of them. One grabbed Alessandro Berardelli, the guard carrying the box. The second pulled a gun and fired three bullets, two into Berardelli and one into Frederick Parmeuter, the paymaster. When the company men staggered to their knees, the gunman pumped three final bullets into the men.

A large Buick glided down the street and pulled to a stop and the two holdup men scrambled into the waiting car and sped off. They roared across a railroad track, brandishing a revolver at a crossing guard who was trying to lower the gate because of an oncoming train. The gunmen left behind them a string of tacks to puncture the tires of any cars that dared follow. They also left the paymaster and the guard dying on the sidewalk under the eyes of more than one hundred horrified onlookers.

The police saw certain similarities between the Bridgewater holdup and the South Braintree murders. A gang of Italian immigrants was probably responsible for the holdups, the police guessed without much evidence. The police were not alone in their suspicion of Italians. In the early 1900s, the textile and shoe factories in Massachusetts employed thousands of immigrants. They came to America expecting better lives, but mostly they found poverty and long hours of dangerous work. Many of them did not speak English and kept to themselves. Old-time residents of New England feared the immigrants might start a revolution and try to overthrow the government like the Communists had in Russia. They especially feared the anarchists, people who rebelled against all government authority. Anarchists organized workers' meetings, led strikes, and published radical literature. Bartolomeo Vanzetti and his good friend Nicola Sacco were anarchists.

Nicola Sacco was the fastest shoe-sole trimmer at the Three-K factory. His boss considered him a model employee, and Sacco served as a night watchman from time to time. He was devoted to his red-haired wife, Rosina, and his infant son, and in the summer he spent hours tending the flower and vegetable garden behind their cottage. He was also devoted to seeking better conditions for his fellow workers. He helped organize a strike at a textile mill, and rose early each morning to walk the picket line before heading off to his own job. He had been at that job on the day of the South Braintree holdup, he later told police investigators.

Both Sacco and Vanzetti had refused to fight in World War I, and in order to escape the draft they had left the United States in 1917 and lived in Mexico. There they became good friends and back in Massachusetts they became active anarchists.

As police began searching for suspects in the two holdups, they focused on certain members of the Italian immigrant community whom they suspected of illegal activity. One

Several eyewitnesses for the prosecution changed their descriptions of Nicola Sacco (left) and Bartolomeo Vanzetti. (UPI/Corbis-Bettmann)

was Mike Boda, a friend of Sacco and Vanzetti who owned a car that matched the description of the getaway car used in the holdups. On the night of May 5, Sacco and Vanzetti went to pick up Boda's car at a garage in Bridgewater. Following a tip-off from the garage owner, the police arrested the two men as they rode a streetcar from Bridgewater to their homes.

Sacco and Vanzetti were clearly nervous when they were arrested by the police. They had good reason to be. Anti-immigrant feeling was running particularly high. Foreigners, especially those from southern and eastern Europe, were seen as especially dangerous. The government, led by U.S. Attorney General A. Mitchell Palmer, had led raids and arrested and deported hundreds of immigrants without issuing proper warrants. Newspapers featured stories warning against possible anarchists' plots to overthrow the government.

Sacco and Vanzetti's friend and fellow radical, Andrea Salsedo, had been arrested in New York, and died in a fall from a fourteen-story window. Authorities called his death a suicide, but others thought he had been murdered by the police. Sacco and Vanzetti were frightened and felt they needed to get rid of their heavy stacks of radical literature. They needed a car for the job and had asked Mike Boda if they could borrow his. Yes, Boda said, but it was in the garage for repairs.

Police were already keeping an eye on the car and had approached the owner of the repair shop for his cooperation.

When Sacco and Vanzetti arrived at the shop to pick up the car, the garage owner told them they should not drive the car since the license plates had expired. Then, as the two men disappeared on foot into the spring evening, he made the fateful call to the police . . . a call that led to the arrest of Sacco and Vanzetti and changed their lives forever.

At the Brockton station, police searched Sacco and found a fully loaded .32 Colt automatic and several live shells. Vanzetti was carrying a loaded .38 caliber Harrington & Richardson revolver and some 12-gauge shotgun shells. Then the questions began.

"Are you a communist? . . . anarchist?" the police chief wanted to know.

"No," Sacco answered.

"Do you believe in this government of ours?"

"Yes," Sacco replied in his imperfect English. "Some things I like different."

"Are you an anarchist?" the chief asked Vanzetti.

"Well, I don't know what you call him. . . . I am a little different," the fish peddler answered.

If a lawyer had been present for Sacco and Vanzetti the two probably would have answered differently, or not at all. But no lawyer was present, nor was one required as one is today. Furthermore, Sacco and Vanzetti did not fully understand English. Frightened and confused, the two thought they had been brought into the station because of their political beliefs or because they had fled to Mexico during the war. Without being told the charges against them, they were locked up in a cell for the night.

It was the county's district attorney, Frederick Katzmann, who took up the questioning the next morning. Where had they been on April 15, the day of the South Braintree killings? Sacco said he thought he had been at work. Vanzetti replied, "Common to every other day to me, I peddled fish."

Katzmann now turned to the Christmas Eve holdup in Bridgewater. Where had the two been that day? At work, Sacco again replied. His boss would confirm that. And how about Vanzetti? Selling fish on the streets, Vanzetti answered. He, however, had no boss to confirm his story.

The questions were over for now, but the long ordeal of Sacco and Vanzetti was only beginning. Vanzetti was charged with "assault with intent to rob" and "assault with intent to murder" in the Bridgewater holdup. In September 1920, both Sacco and Vanzetti were charged with the two murders in the South Braintree robbery. And if they were found guilty, they would go to their deaths in the electric chair.

Vanzetti went on trial alone for the Bridgewater robbery, since Sacco's boss had confirmed he was at work on that day. The trial was conducted by Webster Thayer, a sixty-three-year-old judge with an open distaste for anarchists. Vanzetti's attorney concentrated on his client's alibi and called a series of witnesses who said they had seen Vanzetti selling fish on the streets of Plymouth at the time of the holdup. A baker testified that Vanzetti had asked to borrow his delivery wagon at 7:45 A.M. He remembered the time exactly, he said, because it was the same time the factory whistle blew each morning. Vanzetti's young helper told the court he was with the fish peddler just before eight.

All the witnesses were Italian immigrants. Their English was halting and they were intimidated by the formal courtroom. Through an interpreter, they stumbled nervously over their answers. Vanzetti's former landlady testified that the fish peddler left her house at 6:30 to sell fish on the morning of December 24. In his cross-examination, Katzmann asked her if she remembered what she had done at 7:30 on Christmas morning. No, she answered. What time had Vanzetti gotten up on New Year's Day, on Washington's Birthday? the prosecutor quizzed. "I don't know," she answered. If she remembered Vanzetti's actions of December 24 so accurately, why could she not remember other times and dates as well? the prosecutor challenged.

Another witness insisted he did not speak English.

"Me don't understand you," the witness answered. "You come in my country and you don't understand nothing, and me just the same."

Katzmann then asked the witness to step to the window. "Do you see that team there? What is dragging that team, what is pulling it?"

"A horse," the man answered in English.

The witnesses for Vanzetti left the courtroom shaken and humiliated.

The first prosecution witness was one of the men on the payroll truck. He was "pretty positive" Vanzetti was the gunman, he had said in a preliminary hearing. Now in the courtroom he became more definite. When asked to identify Vanzetti before the jury, he said he was "positive" Vanzetti had done the shooting. It appeared the prosecution had coached their witnesses.

A woman testified she had seen the Bridgewater holdup from a railroad station window a block away. Later, Vanzetti's supporters pointed out the view from that window was completely blocked by a two-story house. A fourteen-year-old boy said he had hidden behind a tree about 145 feet away and saw the man with a shotgun running from the scene of the crime. "I could tell he was a foreigner by the way he ran," the boy said.

The jury deliberated only five and a half hours before delivering a guilty verdict to Judge Thayer. Most criminals convicted of "assault with intent to rob" received 5 to 10 years. Vanzetti received 12 to 15.

The prosecution was now ready to try both Sacco and Vanzetti for the South Braintree murders. The trial was held at the Dedham courthouse. Again, Judge Thayer would serve as the judge. Again, Fred Katzmann would serve as the prosecutor.

By now anarchists in Boston had rallied to Sacco and Vanzetti's cause. They decided the pair needed a new lawyer, and they recommended Fred Moore, a defense attorney who had won many cases for labor agitators and radicals on the West Coast. Moore's courtroom manner was casual. Sometimes he appeared at trials in his stocking feet and on occasion he took naps on the courthouse lawn with a newspaper over his face. He won cases though, and he planned to use Sacco and Vanzetti's political beliefs in court. He was out to prove two proclaimed radicals could be found innocent.

Enthusiastically Moore set up shop in Boston, hired a young, hard-working staff and began a vigorous publicity campaign to gain support for his clients. Soon liberal members of Boston society, many of them women, took up Sacco and Vanzetti's cause, raising money from their wealthy friends for a defense fund. Labor organizations joined in, too.

Days before the trial, the usually quiet streets of Dedham were lined with troopers on horseback. They anticipated protests and demonstrations, but things began quietly. There were only a handful of people in the courtroom — a woman from a Boston church organization, a few reporters from various labor publications, and Rosina Sacco.

The trial began on May 31, 1921, the day after Memorial Day, and patriotic feelings were running high. As the jury filed into the courtroom, the foreman, a retired police chief, stopped to salute the American flag before taking his seat. Next came Sacco and Vanzetti handcuffed and led by marshals to metal cubicles at the front of the courtroom. Fred Katzmann rose to his feet, addressed the judge, and began his argument for the prosecution.

In his best courtroom manner Katzmann reviewed the details of the crime for the jury. There had been witnesses at the scene, he said, witnesses whose testimony would prove Sacco and Vanzetti guilty. One by one Katzmann called them to the stand. One by one they told their damning stories. Suspiciously, though, in the fourteen months since the

South Braintree murders, many of the witnesses' original stories had changed.

Just after the crime, the gatekeeper at the railroad crossing said the man driving the getaway car had called out to him in "clear and unmistakable English." Now in the courtroom, he testified the man had a heavy Italian accent. Earlier he had described the driver's mustache as "short and cropped." Now, seeing Vanzetti in the courtroom, he changed his description to match what he saw. The man in the getaway car had a mustache that was "bushy and droopy," he said.

Even less convincing was the testimony of a second gatekeeper. Vanzetti was clearly the driver of the getaway car, he testified. But, Moore pointed out, Vanzetti did not know

As the appeals for Sacco and Vanzetti dragged on, protestors throughout the world demonstrated against the upcoming execution. (UPI/Corbis-Bettmann)

how to drive a car. Katzmann remained unruffled. What the witness had *really* meant to say was that Vanzetti was a *passenger* in the back of the car, the prosecutor claimed.

To counteract the prosecution witnesses, Moore brought witnesses for the defense. All remembered seeing Vanzetti on April 15, selling fish in Plymouth. There were witnesses for Sacco, too. He was not at work on April 15, he said, because he had gone to Boston to the Italian consulate. He was there to get a passport so he could visit his remaining relatives in Europe. Moore called to the stand a clerk at the consulate. Yes, the clerk testified, he remembered Sacco coming in that day. He had brought a large family photograph for his passport, rather than the small regulation size. There were others, too, who had seen Sacco in Boston that day. They had lunched with him at a restaurant and later joined him in a coffeehouse.

The prosecution, however, brought forward seven witnesses who identified Sacco as one of the bandits in South Braintree. One woman told the court she had been on the second floor of a factory about sixty feet away from the railroad crossing. When she heard the shots, she had run to the window. She had only a fleeting glimpse of the getaway car. Fourteen months later, however, she described in great detail a man she positively identified as Sacco.

"He weighed possibly from 140 to 145 pounds. He was muscular — he was an active-looking man. I noticed particularly the left hand was a good-sized hand, a hand that denoted strength. . . . The face was what we would call clear-cut, clean-cut face. Through here was a little narrow, just a little narrow. The forehead was high. The hair was brushed back and it was between, I should think, two inches and two and one-half inches in length. . . . The complexion was white, a peculiar white that looked greenish." The woman's testimony seemed impossibly detailed for the brief glimpse she had had of the man.

Then there was the issue of the cap. It was found at the crime site and used as evidence during the trial. Katzmann brought it to the courtroom and made Sacco try it on in front of the jury. It perched on top of the defendant's head, obviously too small for him. But the prosecution insisted it had belonged to Sacco. Sacco often hung his cap on a nail at work, his boss at the factory had testified. Look at this, Katzmann pointed out to the jury. There is a slit in the cap's lining. It came from Sacco hanging it each day on that nail in the factory. It was only after the trial a policeman admitted he had cut the cap's lining with scissors before the trial, looking for some sort of identification.

Both the prosecution and the defense brought ballistics experts into court to testify. Witnesses for the defense said definitely that the bullet that killed Alesandro Berardelli had not come from Sacco's Colt. Furthermore, even the two experts for the prosecution were not willing to testify conclusively that the bullet was fired from Sacco's gun. One said there was a "strong similarity" between one of the shells found at the crime scene and test bullets that were fired from Sacco's gun. The second prosecution expert testified he felt the evidence was "consistent with" the bullet having come from Sacco's gun. "Consistent with" meant it was "possible," but it did not mean "positively." Katzmann, however, in his closing statement led the jury to believe the men had said the bullets definitely came from Sacco's gun.

In his cross-examination, Katzmann questioned Sacco's loyalty to America, making the trial a political one rather than a trial for the specific charges against the men. He brought up Sacco's flight to Mexico during the war. "Why didn't you stay down in Mexico?" Katzmann asked Sacco on the stand. ". . . Why didn't you stay down there in that free country and work with a pick and shovel? . . . Is your love for the United States of America commensurate with the amount of money you can get in this country per week?"

"Better conditions, yes," said Sacco.

"Better country to make money, isn't it?" Katzmann continued.

"Yes," said Sacco.

"Is your love for this country measured by the amount of money you can earn here?" Katzmann continued.

"I never loved money," Sacco responded.

Later in his examination Katzmann asked Sacco again to explain what he meant by his love of his country. Sacco's long and disconnected answer did little to win over the jury. "I could see the best men, intelligent, education," he began earnestly. "They been arrested and sent to prison and died in prison for years and years without getting them out. . . ." Sacco then criticized Harvard College, one of the most prized institutions in the state of Massachusetts, as a place available only to the rich. "They won't get, the poor class," he said. "They won't have no chance to go to Harvard College. . . ."

He criticized the war, saying it had been fought for the benefit of rich businessmen. "What right have we to kill each other?" he asked. "I been work for the Irish. I have been working with the German fellow, with the French, many other peoples. I love them people just as I could love my wife. . . . Why should I kill them men? What he done to me? He never done anything, so I don't believe in no war. I want to destroy those guns."

Sacco ended with something that sounded like a call for the overthrow of the government. ". . . You ought to give a chance to socialist literature, education of people, emancipation. That is why I destroy governments, boys. That is why my idea I love socialists."

Sacco's speech inspired his supporters as a genuine statement outlining the beliefs of pacifists and American socialists. The jury, however, heard it as an anarchist's rallying cry for revolution.

On the closing day of the trial, Judge Thayer's desk was covered with flowers from admirers who felt sure Sacco and Vanzetti would be found guilty. In his final instructions to the jury he called on their patriotism. They had responded to their duty "in the spirit of supreme American loyalty," he told them. "There is no better word in the English language than loyalty."

It was three in the afternoon when the jury withdrew for their deliberations. It was a warm summer day and the courtroom was now packed with spectators and journalists anxiously awaiting the verdict. At 7:30 P.M. the jury filed back into the courtroom. The marshal instructed Sacco to stand and look at the jury.

"What say you, Mr. Foreman," the clerk asked. "Is the prisoner at the bar guilty or not guilty?"

"Guilty," the foreman answered.

Vanzetti was next. "Guilty," the foreman announced again. "Guilty of murder in the first degree."

"They kill innocent men," Sacco cried out as he was led from the courtroom. "They kill two innocent men."

For Sacco and Vanzetti, the verdict was devastating, but most Americans paid little attention. The *Boston Herald* openly criticized Judge Thayer and the jury's verdict, but other newspapers ignored or supported the decision. It was Europe that brought the case to the attention of the world. In Rome thousands of workers marched on the American Embassy, and in Paris a protest bomb exploded. Demonstrators gathered in the squares in Brussels and Moscow, and reporters in the United States began looking at the trial more closely. The *New York Times* reported federal agents in Boston had discovered a plot for a nationwide, three-day reign of terror organized by supporters of Sacco and Vanzetti. The country was divided between supporters of the convicted men, those who thought they were guilty, and those who did not know but thought the trial had been unfair.

Fred Moore had filed a motion for a new trial, but Judge

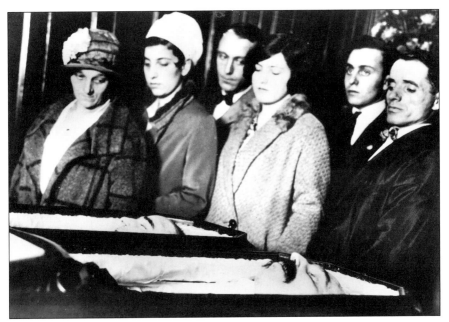

Thousands of mourners viewed the open caskets of Sacco and Vanzetti after their execution. (Underwood & Underwood/Corbis-Bettmann)

Thayer waited until Christmas Eve, two years after the Bridgewater holdup, to deny it. It was only the first in a series of post-trial motions that began a roller coaster of hope, delay, and despair for Sacco and Vanzetti.

After the trial, the two men did not see each other again for six years. They continued to wait out their sentencing, Vanzetti in a Charlestown prison and Sacco in the Dedham jail. Their lawyers visited them and volunteer women from Boston brought them books and gave them English lessons. Sacco, lonely for his wife, started out enthusiastically then sank into a moody despair. Vanzetti, on the other hand, kept busy in the prison shop painting license plates during

17

the day and reading and writing in the evenings. He began work on his autobiography, *The Story of a Proletarian Life*. When he was allowed to visit the Dedham courthouse during one of the appeal hearings he relished being outdoors for a change. In a letter to a friend he wrote, "I observe everything, the trees, the bushes, the grass, the rocks and the brook along the way."

Then suddenly, there was a promising turn of events. At the Dedham jail, a new inmate, convicted for bank robbery, came forward with a startling confession. Sacco and Vanzetti were not responsible for the South Braintree murders, he wrote in a note slipped between the pages of a magazine and smuggled into Sacco's cell. The Morelli gang had done it. He had been with them, drunk in the backseat of the getaway car, when the crime was committed.

Eagerly, attorneys for Sacco and Vanzetti began to track down more information. The Morelli gang was well-known to the police. And a New Bedford policeman had seen Mike Morelli and two other men in a Buick on April 15. Two women identified one of the gang members as one of the strangers they had seen in South Braintree just before the crime occurred. The description of Morelli matched the description of the driver of the getaway car originally given by the gatekeeper at the railroad crossing. Furthermore John Morelli had a .32 Colt, the same type of gun used in the murders.

The defense believed they had an ironclad case. Again they approached Judge Thayer with a motion for a new trial. Again, Thayer refused them. The defense appealed to the Supreme Court, but the higher Court upheld Thayer's decision. The inmate at the Dedham jail probably had confessed in hopes of postponing his own execution date, the judges reasoned.

Sacco and Vanzetti's hopes had been raised and dashed once again. It was now April, and Thayer called the defendants to the Dedham courthouse for sentencing. The pair were to die "by the passage of a current of electricity" through their bodies on July 10, 1927.

Protests erupted throughout the country. Felix Frankfurter, a law professor at Harvard and later a Supreme Court justice, spoke out against what he viewed as unjust treatment by Judge Thayer and Katzmann. Hundreds of famous people joined him. Writers, artists, labor leaders, newspaper columnists, and thousands of others now believed the two immigrants were innocent and called for a new trial.

For a few weeks it seemed there might still be hope for Sacco and Vanzetti. The governor of Massachusetts appointed a high-level advisory committee to review the facts in the case. Late on the night of August 3, the governor read his findings to the press. He and the committee had studied all the evidence, interviewed witnesses, and weighed the matter judicially. "I believe with the jury," his report concluded, "that Sacco and Vanzetti were guilty and that the trial was fair."

The news fell like the blow of a hammer. Busloads of college students, professors, writers, artists, communists, and

The final words of Bartolomeo Vanzetti were captured in a poster by artist Ben Shan. (Library of Congress)

religious leaders poured into Boston. Wearing black arm-bands and carrying placards, they protested in front of the statehouse. Newspapers took up the cause. Protest bombs went off in New York City, Philadelphia, and Baltimore. In Washington, police with riot guns guarded the nation's Capitol building. Mobs stormed American embassies in European cities.

The executions were set for midnight on the night of August 23, 1927. The bridge from Boston to the Charlestown prison was closed, and mounted police lined the barricaded streets around the prison. Mounted machine guns pointed outward from the prison walls. Hundreds of local police and state troopers ringed the prison. In Boston, special pressrooms for reporters were set up with extra phone and telegraph lines. Radio commentators stood ready to broadcast the news to the world.

As evening fell, the searchlights in the prison went on. Shortly after midnight Sacco was led through a green door and into the chamber housing the electric chair. Before the switch was thrown he called out in Italian: "Long live anarchy!" Then, "Farewell my wife and child and all my friends." Within seconds he was dead.

Next, Vanzetti entered, standing tall. He proclaimed his innocence, shook hands with the guards and the warden and then said quietly, "I now wish to forgive some people for what they are doing to me." As the lethal current surged through Vanzetti's body, the warden's eyes filled with tears.

News of the executions flashed through the telegraph wires to cities in Europe, Russia, the Far East, and South

America. Anti-American feelings ran high, riots broke out, and protestors ransacked American embassies and businesses abroad. In Germany six demonstrators were killed and in Paris the city officials brought in tanks to quiet the crowds. For years following the executions American travelers abroad were asked how a country dedicated to democracy could kill two innocent men for simply proclaiming their beliefs.

But questions remained. Were the two really innocent? Some people say that Caro Tresca, an anarchist and vocal supporter of Sacco and Vanzetti, later told a friend, "Sacco was guilty but Vanzetti was innocent." After the trial Fred Moore told friends Sacco was probably guilty and Vanzetti might have been. Some, however, thought Moore said this because he was bitter about being excluded from the appeals process.

Years later the case still raises strong opinions. To some, the two men were anti-American criminals who deserved to die in the electric chair. To others, they represent an unforgivable miscarriage of justice, driven by anti-immigrant feelings and a prejudiced judge. Their supporters continue to be inspired by the words Vanzetti spoke shortly before his death:

If it had not been for this thing, I might have live out my life talking at street corners to scorning men, I might have die, unmarked, unknown, a failure. Now we are not a failure. This is our career and our triumph. Never in our full life can we hope to do such work for tolerance, for justice, for man's understanding of man, as now we do by an accident. Our words — our lives — our pains — nothing! Taking of our lives — lives of a good shoemaker and a poor fish peddler — all! That last moment belongs to us — that agony is our triumph.

2

"YOUR OLD MAN'S
A MONKEY"

THE SCOPES "MONKEY" TRIAL

Every small town has its gathering spot. In Dayton, Tennessee, it was Doc Robinson's drugstore. Nearly all the men in town stopped there sometime during the day to catch up on news and argue about politics. John T. Scopes, the high-school football coach and science teacher, was a regular there.

On a hot May afternoon in 1925, shortly after school had closed, Scopes was playing tennis with a friend. During the set a young boy called to him from the sidelines. The men down at Doc Robinson's wanted to talk to him. Could he come when his game was finished?

After the set was over Scopes casually strolled down to the drugstore, ordered a soda, and pulled a chair up to a table where a group of men sat talking. George Rappelyea, an outspoken and enthusiastic local businessman, asked Scopes if he could teach biology without including the concept of evolution. Not really, Scopes answered.

Robinson's drugstore sold not only sodas but school text-books as well, and Scopes picked up a copy of George Hunter's *Civic Biology* from a nearby shelf. The book had been approved by the state textbook commission six years earlier and was used in classrooms all over Tennessee. He opened the book to the chart showing the evolution of man from early apes and a passage explaining Charles Darwin's theory of evolution.

Did Scopes use the book? Rappelyea asked him. Yes, Scopes said, he had used Hunter's book that spring when he was helping students review for exams. Then he had broken the law, Doc Robinson told him.

Scopes was familiar with the law. It was the Butler Act, passed earlier that year by the state legislature: It outlawed the teaching of evolution. The bill had pitted religious fun-damentalists against evolutionists. Many of the mountain people in the Cumberland hills near Dayton were funda-mentalists. Scraping a living from the poor mountain soil took much of their time, and they had little interest in edu-cation and were cut off from outside ideas. They did not *think* about religion, they *felt* it. The fundamentalists be-lieved every word in the Bible was true. God created the earth and humans in just six days, the Bible told them, and they accepted the story without question.

Still, no one in Dayton had taken the anti-evolution bill very seriously. Even Tennessee governor Austin Peay had said, "Probably the law will never be applied. Nobody believes that it is going to be an active statute." Why, Scopes wondered, did the people of Dayton suddenly care about how biology was taught in their schools?

Then Rappelyea showed Scopes an ad placed in the May 4 issue of the *Chattanooga Daily Times* by the American Civil Liberties Union. The ACLU, a New York organization which defended people's constitutional rights, was alarmed by Tennessee's anti-evolution law. The Constitution of the United States guaranteed freedom of religion. If other states passed similar laws, the right of Americans to think freely would be in peril, the group believed. The ACLU was looking for someone willing to be arrested for teaching evolution, then stand trial. In exchange the organization would provide money for top-flight defense lawyers.

The city fathers of Dayton saw the ACLU offer as a good opportunity for the city. Business had been slow in Dayton since the coal and iron mills in the surrounding region had closed. A major trial, pitting evolutionists against fundamentalists, would bring hundreds of newsmen and spectators to Dayton. The men at Robinson's wanted that trial in their town. Was Scopes willing to stand trial in a test case? Doc Robinson asked Scopes. Without a great deal of thought the shy, red-haired teacher said yes. He had been raised to stand up for what he thought was right and if convicted, he would probably only be required to pay a small fine.

If Scopes had known, however, on that May afternoon that his name would soon appear in newspaper headlines

William Jennings Bryan, an eloquent orator, ran unsuccessfully for U.S. president several years before the Scopes trial. (Corbis-Bettmann)

throughout the world, he never would have agreed to stand trial. He did not like being in the limelight. In Dayton Scopes was popular among his students, and he was content with his quiet, small-town life. But once he said yes to the men at Robinson's, his private life was over.

Scopes never wanted to be a hero in the evolution case. There were others, however, who did. William Jennings Bryan was considered the greatest public speaker in America. His rich baritone voice spellbound thousands of listeners, and he had campaigned vigorously for the causes of peace, the poor, women's rights, and religion. As a lawyer in Lincoln, Nebraska, Bryan became the spokesman of the farmers and miners of the West and Midwest. He was stoutly religious and the fundamentalists loved him. Bryan ran for president on the Democratic ticket three times, and lost three times. Woodrow Wilson appointed him secretary of state, but from the beginning it was clear Bryan was not cut out for the job.

At age sixty-five Bryan was a disappointed politician, living in Florida where he taught Sunday school. He loved to eat and was dangerously overweight. A companion during one of his presidential campaigns described what Bryan had eaten one morning for breakfast — a cantaloupe, two quails, Virginia ham, six eggs, two helpings of pancakes, fried potatoes, and coffee. He now suffered from diabetes, but when he heard of the Scopes case he geared up for a good fight and offered to represent the fundamentalists at the Dayton trial.

Now the fundamentalists had in their corner one of the most famous, most eloquent men in America. But while Bryan had hundreds of thousands of supporters, there were others who saw him as a narrow-minded bigot. One of his critics was Clarence Darrow, a brilliant defense lawyer from Chicago. Like Scopes and Bryan, Darrow had grown up poor in a small town. He had studied all the world's religions and had read the Bible and everything Darwin had ever written. He was appalled by the fundamentalists' disregard of science and their efforts to impose their religious beliefs on America's school system.

When Darrow heard of the Scopes trial, he was interested. When he heard that Bryan was to be the lead prosecutor, there was no holding him back. Within hours, he telegraphed the ACLU offering his services for the defense.

Back in Tennessee, the people of Dayton were delighted. Bryan was a national celebrity and his religious views were popular in the area. Darrow was a brilliant courtroom lawyer. The two were bound to create headlines and draw huge crowds to town. And H.L. Mencken, a cocky young journalist from Baltimore, wanted to write those headlines. Mencken was known throughout the United States as a talented, but irreverent, reporter. He took particular pleasure in ridiculing the South and what he considered its backward ideas. He called Tennessee and surrounding states the "Bible Belt" and dubbed the upcoming Scopes trial the "Monkey Trial." Even those who thought he was arrogant and insulting to small-town America regularly read his weekly column for the *Baltimore Sun* and his monthly article in the *American Mercury* magazine. Bryan, Darrow, and Mencken were an unbeatable cast of characters. The stage was now set in Dayton for a spectacular show. And John Scopes was rapidly becoming a bystander in his own trial.

Even before the trial began, the streets of Dayton were filled with vendors selling hot dogs, sandwiches, and lemonade. Stores sold monkey dolls, monkey pins, and posters proclaiming "Your Old Man's a Monkey." At Robinson's, customers now ordered Monkey Fizzes instead of sodas. The Anti-Evolution League set up an open-air bookstall. Religious sects from all over the South swarmed into town, preaching on street corners and setting up revival meetings in tents outside of town. A circus man displayed two live chimpanzees in a shop window on Main Street and mountain men came down from the hills to play their fiddles and sing gospel hymns.

Business was booming in Dayton. The local hotel upped its prices to eight dollars a night, and townspeople happily rented rooms to the thousands of fundamentalists, newsmen, photographers, and farmers who thronged into town. Those who could not find lodging in hotels or homes camped out, sleeping in wagons or tents or under their cars. New phone lines were installed and Western Union operators, who would telegraph news of the trial to papers around the world, set up shop in a room above the local hardware store.

Dayton had become a circus and everyone was waiting for the performers to arrive. On July 7, almost the whole town crowded into the railroad depot to watch the *Royal Palm Express* from Florida puff into the train station. It carried William Jennings Bryan, and when the famous orator emerged onto the platform at the back of the train, a welcoming cheer went up. Age and overeating had taken their toll on Bryan, and he was pale and jowly. But he still had a charismatic charm, and to the eager crowd in Dayton he appeared a champion and hero. In spite of the overwhelming heat, he looked distinguished in his pinstriped pants and his black jacket. Excitedly the townspeople drove him through Dayton in an open car, down the main street strung with banners urging READ YOUR BIBLE, PREPARE TO MEET YOUR GOD, and JESUS IS COMING.

Later, Bryan strolled downtown in his shirtsleeves, talking with locals and enjoying a soda at Robinson's. He introduced himself to John Scopes and the two exchanged a friendly handshake. He wore a pith helmet, a souvenir from his recent trip to the jungles of Panama, to protect his balding head from the sun. He was altogether charming and at ease in these small-town surroundings. "This is the day I have been waiting for," he told his assembled admirers. "The contest between evolution and Christianity is a duel to the death. If evolution wins in Dayton, Christianity goes."

If Bryan was Dayton's hero, Clarence Darrow was at least an honored guest. At a dinner given for him he said, "I was born in a little town like this one. . . . I went to school for a while, and then I quit school and started my education." His easygoing, friendly manner soon made him a favorite with everyone he met. He and his wife, Ruby, were treated with southern hospitality. Even Mencken, who wandered the streets in his straw-brimmed hat, baiting fundamentalists and ridiculing their beliefs, described Dayton as "a county town full of charm and beauty."

The heat, however, was not part of Dayton's charm. On the opening day of the trial, July 10, hundreds of sweltering spectators climbed the wooden stairs to the huge courtroom on the second floor of the Rhea County Courthouse. Seven hundred onlookers squeezed onto the newly varnished wooden benches and another three hundred stood in the back, their sleeves rolled up, the shotguns of the mountain men propped against the walls. More than two hundred reporters sat ready to scribble notes to phone back to their

Clarence Darrow (leaning on table) in his shirtsleeves due to the blistering heat in the courtroom. John Scopes, seated at the table behind him, listens attentively. (Library of Congress)

papers. A radio commentator set up his microphones to broadcast the trial to the country. Radio was new, and this was a first for the broadcasters and their listeners.

At the front of the room, William Jennings Bryan sat, coatless, his shirt collar unbuttoned, fanning himself with a palm-leaf fan as he moved back and forth in a large rocker. With him at the prosecutors' table were his son, William Jennings Bryan, Jr., who was an attorney in California, and Tennessee's attorney general, William Stewart.

Darrow, slightly rumpled and sporting bright blue suspenders, sat at the defense table next to Scopes. Dudley Field

Malone, a lawyer for the ACLU, was there, too, looking cool and distinguished in a dark, double-breasted suit.

At nine-thirty, Judge John Tate Raulston arrived and took his place behind the bench. He called the court to order, then did something that enraged Darrow: He asked a fundamentalist minister to open the proceedings with a prayer. Already Darrow sensed this Tennessee courtroom would not be sympathetic to any case challenging the local views on religion and education.

In selecting the jury, the defense found they were limited to men unlikely to be sympathetic to their case, but Darrow was satisfied with anyone he thought would listen to reason. The twelve men finally chosen reflected the values of the Tennessee rural community. They were eager to serve since it would guarantee them a front-row seat for the trial. John Scopes knew all the men on the jury and later said, "It was safe to assume that I had an excellent chance of being convicted."

Friday afternoon the judge adjourned the court and people poured into the steaming streets of Dayton. The defense team gathered at the mansion where they had set up headquarters and, as Darrow lounged on a bed, plotted their strategy for the trial. Bryan wandered through town carrying a bag full of radishes, one of his favorite between-meals snacks, and consulted with Stewart and other members of the prosecution. Meanwhile H.L. Mencken strolled the streets of Dayton watching the goings-on and interviewing locals. Mencken had invented a mythical Dayton character named Elmer Chubb for his articles and took delight in ridiculing what he considered the backward ways of the "yokels" who congregated on every street corner.

Monday morning the Dayton courthouse was still stifling. Spectators fluttered their cardboard fans. Some actually fainted from heat prostration as Bryan sat silent and stern-faced in his rocker. Darrow chomped on a cigar and wore a shirt with an obvious hole in it.

The two opposing attorneys had once been friends. Darrow had even campaigned for Bryan the first two times he ran for president. But now the two were archenemies and they were prepared for battle. Bryan was there to defend the faith, to prove that fundamentalists were the only Christians who spoke for God. Darrow, on the other hand, was there to champion the cause of knowledge and evolution. "Scopes is not on trial," he said. "Civilization is on trial."

As the spectators in the courtroom settled into their seats Dudley Malone opened for the defense, arguing that the Butler Act was unconstitutional. It was a violation of separation of church and state, he told the court. The state of Tennessee had a right to pass any law they wanted to, Attorney General Stewart responded, and the locals in the courtroom nodded in agreement.

Then Darrow rose to his feet and sauntered to the front of the courtroom. He looked very much like a country lawyer from the hills of Tennessee. The crowd leaned forward. Darrow might look like one of theirs, but everyone in the courtroom knew his reputation as an agnostic. "There was a craning of necks, for Mr. Darrow is of intense interest hereabout," a reporter for the *New York Times* wrote. "He is known as 'the infidel,' and the crowd gazed curiously at the bent figure with the seamed brown face and the great head."

Darrow began by questioning Tennessee's right to decide what should be taught in its schools. Under the Constitution, the state has "no more right to teach the Bible as the divine book than that the Koran is one, or the book of Mormons or the book of Confucius or the Buddha," he reasoned in his chatty style.

He questioned the fundamentalists' view of the Bible. "The Bible is made up of sixty-six books written over a period of about one thousand years. . . . It is a book primarily of religion and morals. It is not a book of science. Never was and was never meant to be.

"You cannot jail a man just because his opinions are different from your own," he told the attentive crowd. "Your life and my life and the life of every American citizen depends after all upon the tolerance and forbearance of his fellow man. If men are not tolerant, if men cannot respect each other's opinions, if men cannot live and let live, then no man's life is safe," he told them.

Darrow went on to set the stage for what might happen if the Butler Act were carried out to its fullest. Banning books and newspapers might well follow on the heels of banning the teaching of evolution, he told them.

Darrow's listeners were spellbound. How could such a down-home, engaging man speak so eloquently about such heretical ideas, they wondered. He was brilliant, and when the court adjourned a crowd of admirers thronged around him. Even Attorney General Stewart threw his arm around him and said, "That was the greatest speech I have ever heard on any subject in my life." Darrow's wife, however, was more concerned about the hole in his shirt. He should put on another one, she told him. "Well, Ruby," he responded with good humor, "don't you think it's a little hot for two shirts?"

Darrow was feeling confident when he entered the court on Tuesday, but he lost much of the respect he had gained the day before when he formally objected to the opening prayers in the courtroom. The judge and the spectators were stunned. Clearly Darrow did not understand the importance of religion in Tennessee. Public prayers were a part of their daily lives.

Then he argued with Judge Raulston about expert witnesses. He had arranged for some of the country's most intelligent scientists and religious experts to testify during the trial, but Judge Raulston did not want the jury to hear their testimony since he thought it would prejudice them. He refused to rule on whether Darrow's witnesses would be allowed to testify in the presence of the jury.

The next day the prosecution called three of Scopes's former high school students to testify. They readily admitted John Scopes had taught them about evolution. Darrow cross-examined one of the boys in a friendly, easygoing manner.

"Now, he [Scopes] said the earth was once a molten mass of liquid, didn't he?"

"Yes, sir."

"After that, after it got cooled enough, and the soil came, that the plants grew, is that right?" Darrow asked.

"Yes, sir."

"And that the first life was in the sea? And that it developed into life on the land?"

"Yes, sir."

"And finally into the highest organism, which is known as man?"

"Yes, sir."

"It has not hurt you any, has it?"

"No, sir."

The next witness, a seventeen-year-old, told the court that Scopes had taught him that all life came from a single cell.

"Are you a church member?" Darrow asked him.

"Yes, sir."

"Do you still belong?"

"Yes, sir."

"You didn't leave church when he told you all forms of life began with a single cell?"

"No, sir."

Finally Darrow called Dr. Maynard Metcalf, a professor of zoology from Johns Hopkins University, to the stand. Metcalf, a highly religious man, had taught courses in the Bible and had been a deacon in his church. He was about to launch into his testimony when Judge Raulston interrupted him to excuse the jury from the room. Metcalf could testify, but only for the record, the judge said. The twelve men obediently filed out of the courtroom and took seats on the lawn along with hundreds of spectators. The jurors were still able to hear Metcalf's testimony, however, over loudspeakers set up outside.

Led by Darrow's questioning Metcalf began his explanation of evolution. Evolution, he said, meant change. ". . . it means the change of an organism from one character into a different character." Judge Raulston leaned forward and the people in the courtroom listened attentively as Metcalf explained that early life had begun on earth more than six hundred million years ago.

Bryan still sat silent, rocking and fanning while Attorney General Stewart attacked the defense's arguments. "They want to put words into God's mouth," Stewart told the court, "and have Him say that He issued some sort of protoplasm, or soft dishrag, and put it in the ocean and said, 'Old boy, if you wait about six thousand years I will make something out of you.'" The spectators laughed in appreciation.

The courtroom audience, however, was restless to hear from Bryan. Finally on Thursday afternoon, with ceiling fans installed in the hope of making the room more bearable, the revered attorney rose to his feet and approached the bench. More spectators crammed into the already packed courtroom and outside the growing crowd on the lawn waited expectantly under the loudspeakers.

Bryan, his shirtsleeves rolled, turned his back to the judge and addressed the spectators as if they were one of his religious audiences. Immediately he won them over. "The Bible

Young John Scopes (center) flanked by his two lead defense attorneys, Dudley Malone (left) and Clarence Darrow. (UPI/Corbis-Bettmann)

is the word of God," he intoned. "The Bible is the only expression of man's hope of salvation. . . . That Bible is not going to be driven out of this court by experts who come hundreds of miles to testify that they can reconcile evolution with its ancestor in the jungle.

"The Christian believes man came from above," Bryan told his rapt listeners, "but the Evolutionist believes he must have come from below, that is, from a lower order of animals." If children are taught about evolution they will go home and "scoff at the religion of their parents," he continued. He concluded with a thundering criticism of these people who "come in from outside of the state and force upon the people of this state" their own view of morality. The exuberant crowd rose to their feet and thronged around Bryan to shake his hand, thanking him for his eloquent defense of their beliefs. He was their hero, and he had not disappointed them.

It was Dudley Malone, not Darrow, who responded to Bryan. He began quietly, then built his case and increased his volume. "Mr. Bryan," he told the court, "is not the only one who believes in God; he is not the only one who believes in the Bible."

He appealed to the parents in the courtroom to trust their children's good judgment. "We have no fears about the young people of America. They are a pretty smart generation." They should be able to learn all the facts and theories available, Malone said. "Are we to have our children know nothing about science except what the church says they shall know?" he questioned.

"There are millions of people who believe in evolution and in the stories of creation as set forth in the Bible and who find no conflict between the two." The people in the courtroom leaned forward with interest. "Keep your Bible. Keep it as your consolation, keep it as your guide," he told them. "But keep it where it belongs, in the world of your own conscience." The packed courtroom listened with respect.

Finally Malone closed with a ringing plea for education.

". . . we do not fear all the truth. . . . We feel we stand with progress. We feel we stand with science. We feel we stand with intelligence. We feel we stand with fundamental freedom in America. We are not afraid. Where is the fear? We meet it! Where is the fear? We defy it!"

When Malone was through speaking, the audience went wild, cheering and pounding the floor in appreciation. Only Bryan sat silently, staring straight ahead. "Dudley," he told his former employee as the crowd dispersed, "that was the greatest speech I have ever heard."

"Thank you, Mr. Bryan," Malone replied with gentle courtesy. "I am sorry it was I who had to make it."

After Bryan's speech and Malone's rebuttal many of the reporters packed their bags and left town. The sidewalk vendors and preachers disappeared from the streets of Dayton and interest in the Scopes trial began to wane. The show, however, was not over.

Monday morning brought no relief from Dayton's scalding heat wave and the courtroom was filled with perspiring spectators and buzzing flies. By two o'clock on Tuesday, the heat in the courtroom was almost sickening. The floor of the old building creaked and groaned ominously under the weight of the hundreds of people there, and Judge Raulston decided to move the trial to the lawn outside. The crowd on the courthouse lawn was delighted. At last they could actually see the great men up close. Boys climbed trees, stood on car tops, and balanced on fences to see over the throngs that crowded around the platform.

Bryan had his rocker brought outside and he settled himself comfortably into it, his palm-leaf fan in his hand. He appeared relaxed under the arching elm trees surrounded by a curious and reverent audience. Darrow, contentious as ever, objected to the judge about the large banner stating READ YOUR BIBLE that was strung across the courthouse lawn. After a heated argument Darrow said he did not mind if it stayed up as long as the defense could hang a banner saying READ YOUR EVOLUTION. At the judge's order the sign came down.

Then came an unexpected and dramatic request.

"The defense desires to call Mr. Bryan as a witness."

Immediately the prosecution lawyers leapt to their feet to object. Bryan himself looked startled, then agreed and took a seat on a small wooden stool facing Darrow.

Darrow eased Bryan into a series of questions in his traditional, friendly manner. He was a serious student of the Bible, wasn't he? Darrow asked Bryan. Yes, for fifty years, Bryan answered comfortably.

"Do you claim that everything in the Bible should be literally interpreted?"

"I believe everything in the Bible should be accepted as it is given there," Bryan replied.

Darrow then questioned him about the Old Testament story of Jonah being swallowed by a whale. Did Bryan believe that actually happened? "I believe it, and I believe in a God who can make a whale and can make a man and make them both do what he pleases," said Bryan.

How about the story of Joshua making the sun stand still?

Did he believe that? "I believe what the Bible says," Bryan replied stoutly.

Darrow plowed ahead. "Do you believe at that time the entire sun went around the earth?"

"No, I believe the earth goes around the sun," Bryan said, giving the accepted scientific answer.

Was it the sun that stood still or the earth? Darrow questioned. It might have been the earth, Bryan answered, becoming confused and rattled by the rapid-fire questions. And what might have happened if the earth stood still? Darrow demanded to know. I believe God could have taken care of that, Bryan responded, refusing to be drawn into dangerous territory.

Bryan's composure was rapidly disappearing as Darrow led him into a minefield of contradictions, memory lapses, and nervous responses. When did the Bible say the great flood took place? he questioned his perspiring witness.

"I would not attempt to fix the day."

"But what do you think that the Bible itself says?"

"I never made a calculation."

"What do *you* think?"

"I do not think about things I don't think about."

"Do you think about things you *do* think about?"

Even Bryan's supporters burst into laughter at this admission, and Bryan turned to glower at them. As Darrow grew more argumentative and irrational in his questioning, Bryan grew grimmer and more stubborn. Darrow barked out a series of questions about Buddha, Zoroaster, and Confucius, in an attempt to display Bryan's ignorance of other religions.

He quizzed him about his knowledge of ancient cultures and religions. Bryan conceded he had never studied them. Then came the clincher.

"Do you think the earth was made in six days?" Darrow questioned.

"Not six days of twenty-four hours," Bryan answered.

The audience was stunned. The Bible said God made the earth in six days, and now Bryan was saying he did not believe it.

Darrow's hostile questions were flying fast and furiously now and Bryan's testy answers grew more heated. Finally the two were shouting at each other, oblivious to the crowd on the lawn. Judge Raulston had finally had enough. Court was adjourned for the day, he declared. An admiring crowd swarmed around Darrow, leaving Bryan with only one friend and looking fatigued and defeated.

Darrow had clearly won the day, but it was a bittersweet victory. He had exposed Bryan and the fundamentalists as naive, unthinking, and out of touch. But in the process, he had destroyed a great hero. "Bryan was broken, if ever a man was broken," wrote a reporter for a St. Louis newspaper. "Darrow never spared him. It was masterly, but it was pitiful."

The next day Judge Raulston made two rulings. Bryan's testimony from the day before was to be stricken from the record. And Bryan was not to take the stand again. The judge gave the jury final instructions. The jury had only to rule on whether or not John Scopes had violated the Butler Act by teaching evolution. Darrow, in his remarks, asked that the twelve men find Scopes guilty. If they did, he reasoned, the case could be appealed to the state's supreme court and the defense would once again have an opportunity to try to prove the law unconstitutional.

The jury obligingly delivered a guilty verdict, and while Scopes stood shyly at the front of the courtroom, his head down, Judge Raulston fined him one hundred dollars. In closing the case Raulston told the court, "A man who is big enough to search for the truth and find it and declare it in the face of all opposition is a big man."

By evening, the circus in Dayton was folding its tent and leaving town. Darrow and his wife headed for the nearby Smoky Mountains to relax with friends. On Sunday, Bryan made a speech in a town near Dayton, calling on his

Clarence Darrow nails home a point during the "Monkey Trial." (UPI/ Corbis-Bettmann)

audience to continue the fight against evolution in the schools. He would continue the fundamentalists' fight, he assured them. But even his wife gently cautioned him to remember the constitutional guarantee of religious freedom.

The heat had not abated and Bryan was weary from the ordeal he had just endured. When he and his wife reached Dayton he ate one of his enormous meals, then went to their room for an afternoon nap. He never awoke, having died in his sleep.

When Darrow heard the news he and his wife returned to Dayton, facing accusations by some reporters that it was his brutal questioning that caused Bryan to die of a broken heart. "His death is a great loss to the American people," Darrow told the reporters. Under his breath, however, he muttered, "Broken heart nothing; he died of a busted belly."

A year after the trial in Dayton, the Tennessee State Supreme Court heard the appeal and reversed the lower court's ruling on a technicality. As for the constitutionality of the Butler Anti-Evolution Act, two judges found it constitutional, three found it irrelevant to the Scopes case, and one judge found it unconstitutional. "There is always one," Darrow declared with hope.

It was not until the 1970s, however, that anti-evolution laws in other states were declared unconstitutional by the Supreme Court. By then few remembered the fiery exchange in Dayton. Shortly after the trial, John Scopes left Dayton for graduate school at the University of Chicago and spent most of his life as a geologist. While his name was indelibly printed in the memories of millions he himself lived a quiet, uneventful life with his wife and children.

Darrow went on to try a few more cases before he retired completely, but the Scopes case had been his final triumph. There were those in Dayton, however, who would never forgive him for his treatment of Bryan. But Darrow took pride in having fought for the cause of religious tolerance and freedom of thought in public education. And to his great delight the young people of Dayton regarded him as a hero and held a dance in his honor on his last night in town — at the very high school where the Scopes controversy had begun.

3

BABY CHARLES AND

THE CARPENTER

THE LINDBERGH BABY KIDNAPPING TRIAL

The young couple seemed to live a charmed life. "Lindy," Charles Lindbergh, Sr., a handsome, boyish aviator, became a national hero when he flew solo from New York to Paris in 1927. He was the first pilot to cross the Atlantic. His wife, Anne Morrow Lindbergh, was the daughter of a wealthy, prominent banking family. She wrote poetry and flew with Lindy on his daring missions. They had wealth, exciting lives, and the adoration of the world. They also had a son, Charles Lindbergh, Jr., a blond, blue-eyed toddler. Lindy was the Eagle; Charley was the Eaglet.

Then, on March 1, 1932, the Lindberghs' world came crashing down.

Anne and her eighteen-month-old son were staying at Highfields, the Lindberghs' estate in New Jersey. Usually, the two would have been with Anne's mother at her nearby estate, Next Day Hill, where the Lindberghs stayed during the week. But little Charley had a cold, and his mother decided he should not travel. She called Next Day Hill and asked Betty Gow, the boy's nursemaid, to come to Highfields to help out with the baby.

Gow was not happy about coming. She had a date that night with a Norwegian sailor named Red Johnson, and she wanted to be with him rather than working. But she was a loyal employee and asked the Morrow family chauffeur to drive her to Highfields.

At Charley's bedtime his mother and Gow gave him a bath. Then his nanny stitched up a tiny nightshirt for him, cut from an old flannel gown he had outgrown, to wear under his Dr. Denton sleeping suit. It would protect him from the night chill, she told his mother. The two women closed the windows in his room against the blustery wind blowing outside, leaving one open just a crack for fresh air. By eight o'clock the baby was asleep in his crib. His mother went downstairs to wait for her husband to arrive home from his day in New York City. Betty Gow went upstairs to chat with Mrs. Whateley, the butler's wife.

About eight o'clock, Charles Lindbergh arrived home. He and Anne ate a late dinner then went into the living room to read. While there they heard a crash. One of the servants had dropped something in the pantry, they thought, ignoring the sound. Later they went upstairs to get ready for bed.

At 10:00 Betty Gow left Mrs. Whateley's room and slipped back into the nursery to check on young Charley. She stepped across the darkened room and felt for the baby's tiny body in the crib. But the crib was empty. Baby Charles

Handwriting experts found Hauptmann's writing and spelling similar to those in the ransom note left at the scene of the kidnapping. (Library of Congress) was not there. Surely, she thought, his parents must have him. She hurried down the hall and knocked on the Lindberghs' bedroom door. The two looked at her blankly. No, they said, the baby was not with them. He's gone, she told them. Wildly the three searched the nursery, the closet, under the crib. The baby was nowhere to be found.

As the terrifying reality set in, Charles Lindbergh shouted to a servant to call the police, then grabbed his rifle and ran outside. In the windy dark, he searched the grounds, but finding no one, he hurried back to the house and up to the nursery. His heart sank as he spied a white envelope lying on top of the radiator.

"Dear Sir!" it read. "Have 50,000 $ redy 25000 $ in 20 $ bills 15000 $ in 10 $ bills and 10000 $ in 5 $ bills. After 2-4 days we will inform you were to deliver the mony. We warn you for making anyding public or for notify the polise The child is in gut care. Indication for all letters are singnature and 3 holds."

The "singnature" was two overlapping circles outlined in blue on the outside, filled in with red in the center. The "3 holds" were three square holes made with a hand punch.

Within minutes of receiving a call the local and state police arrived at the Highfields estate. Under the nursery window they discovered muddy footprints. Farther away from the house they found a crude ladder, roughly nailed together from planks of used wood. One of its bottom rungs was broken.

At the news of the kidnapping, news reporters, photographers, and hundreds of spectators flocked to Highlands.

New phone lines installed in the house rang constantly, and thousands of letters offering sympathy and advice arrived each day in the mail. Newspapers splashed Lindbergh kidnapping headlines across their front pages, and radio stations issued hourly bulletins. A plane buzzed over Highfields, carrying spectators who had paid the pilot $2.50 each to view the Lindbergh estate from the air.

Days passed and the police still had not come up with any serious leads. The Lindberghs, frantic for the return of their son, turned to a riskier source of help, a man named Mickey Rosner. Rosner was known to have a criminal record and claimed the baby had been taken by a group of gangsters. He had contacts with the underworld, he bragged, and he could arrange for the child's return. It was weeks before the Lindberghs realized Rosner was a con man with no information about their baby.

Meanwhile, Betty Gow had struck up a conversation with one of the New Jersey policemen investigating the case. She told him of breaking her date with Red Johnson the afternoon before the kidnapping. He had called her that night at Highfields about eight-thirty, she confided. The New Jersey police thought they finally had a real lead. Since Johnson was Norwegian he probably did not write English very well and might have written the poorly spelled ransom note. And, of course, Betty Gow knew all the details of the Lindbergh household. Probably the two were in on the plot together, the police reasoned.

The New Jersey police tracked down Red Johnson and

arrested him, but Johnson told the police of his activities the night of the kidnapping, and his story checked out. The New Jersey police had arrested the wrong man and were humiliated by their mistake.

In Washington, D.C., a wealthy socialite named Evalyn Walsh McLean received a message from Gaston Means, a detective with a criminal record. He had had contact with the Lindbergh kidnap gang, he told her, and if she would hand over to him one hundred thousand dollars he would arrange for the baby's safe return. Trustingly, McLean gave him the money, then followed him on a long and fruitless chase from Maryland to South Carolina, Texas, and Mexico. McLean finally realized she had been duped and Gaston Means was arrested and found guilty of larceny and embezzlement. Her money was never returned.

People who had never met the Lindberghs considered the crime their own personal case to solve. One such person was Dr. John Condon, a former school principal from the Bronx. He ran an advertisement in a neighborhood newspaper offering to act as the contact person between the kidnappers and the Lindberghs. No one took him seriously until he telephoned the Highfields estate. He had received a note in response to his ad, he reported. Many of the words were misspelled and there was a strange symbol at the bottom of the note — two interlocking circles outlined in blue, filled in with red. Before nightfall, Dr. Condon was on his way to Highfields.

The note he handed to Colonel Lindbergh read: "after

you gett the Mony from Mr. Lindbergh put them 3 word's in the New York *American* money is redy." At Lindbergh's instruction Condon placed an ad in the New York *American*. He signed it "Jasfie," a false name he adopted for himself. A few days later, a cab driver arrived at the door of Condon's Bronx apartment. He had with him a note addressed to "Jasfie." Go to a frankfurter stand on Jerome Avenue in the Bronx, the note said. There Condon found a second note directing him to Woodlawn Cemetery several blocks away.

Just as twilight was settling over the Bronx, Condon and a friend drove toward the gloomy meeting place. It was dark by the time they arrived at the high iron fence enclosing the graveyard. As Condon got out of the car and cautiously approached the locked gate, he saw a man walking toward him waving a white handkerchief. His name was "John," the stranger told Condon in a heavy German accent, and he wanted the ransom money. Not yet, Condon replied. He needed proof from John that the baby was all right. Could he produce an article of the baby's clothing? John was evasive. It would take a while, he said. Four days later a package arrived at Condon's apartment. A tiny woolen sleeping outfit was folded inside. It belonged to his son, Charles Lindbergh told Condon when he saw the freshly laundered suit.

Eager for the return of his son Lindbergh decided it was time to deliver the ransom money. At the house of Morgan, the New York banking firm where Anne Morrow Lindbergh's father had amassed his fortune, federal agents from the Treasury Department assembled a huge package of five-, ten-, and twenty-dollar gold notes. Gold notes, or certificates, were paper currency issued by banks. They were used just like any other paper money, but Lindbergh and his advisors thought they would be easier to trace, since there were fewer of them in circulation. Meticulously, the agents noted down the serial numbers for each bill.

The evening of April 2, one month after the baby's kidnapping, Colonel Lindbergh, his attorney, and Dr. Condon waited nervously in the living room of Condon's Bronx apartment. At eight, a cab driver again knocked on the door and handed Condon a note instructing him to drive to a Bronx florist's shop where he would find another note. Lindbergh, a pistol concealed in a shoulder holster under his suit jacket, drove with Condon. The wooden box containing the ransom money lay on the seat between them. At the florist's shop they found a second note hidden under a stone. "Cross the street," it read. "Come alone."

In the dark, Condon left Lindbergh in the car and crossed Whitmore Avenue to St. Raymond's Cemetery. As he approached the entrance, a voice called out "Hey, Doctor." Condon recognized the heavy German accent immediately. It was "Graveyard John." Lindbergh, waiting in the car several yards away, heard the voice, too.

Condon entered the cemetery and followed the shadowy figure along a winding dirt path. Then, surrounded by gravestones and heavy bushes, Condon handed John the box filled with ransom money. John opened it and inspected the contents, then pulled an envelope from his pocket and handed it to Condon. Back in the car, Lindbergh and Condon tore open the note and read the scrawled message:

"The boy is on the Boad Nelly. . . . You will find the Boad between Horseneck Beach and Gay Head on Elizabeth Island."

Lindbergh was ecstatic. He knew the location. It was off the coast of Cape Cod, where he and Anne had vacationed. Within hours Lindy had borrowed a small plane and collected a blanket, diapers, and a baby bottle, convinced he would soon be reunited with his son. Together with his attorney and Condon, he took off from a Connecticut airstrip. Back at the Highfields estate the light was on in the nursery again as Anne expectantly awaited the return of her baby.

Lindbergh and his passengers reached the Elizabeth Islands early on Sunday morning. In the brilliant cool spring sun they flew low over the fishing and pleasure boats bobbing in the waves below. For hours they searched the coastline for a boat named Nelly, but as the hours passed their excitement turned to despair. They had been fooled, they realized with sinking hearts. Graveyard John had the ransom money, but the baby was still missing.

Desperate, Lindy turned to another lead. John Hughes Curtis, a marina owner, had contacted the Lindberghs and told them he had met with the kidnapping gang and had seen the ransom money. They were holding the baby on a small sailing schooner called the *Mary B. Moss* anchored off the coast of New Jersey, he said. Lindbergh and his com-

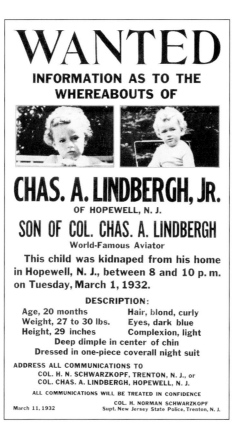

WANTED

INFORMATION AS TO THE WHEREABOUTS OF

CHAS. A. LINDBERGH, JR.

OF HOPEWELL, N. J.

SON OF COL. CHAS. A. LINDBERGH

World-Famous Aviator

This child was kidnaped from his home in Hopewell, N. J., between 8 and 10 p. m. on Tuesday, March 1, 1932.

DESCRIPTION:

Age, 20 months   Hair, blond, curly
Weight, 27 to 30 lbs.   Eyes, dark blue
Height, 29 inches   Complexion, light
Deep dimple in center of chin
Dressed in one-piece coverall night suit

ADDRESS ALL COMMUNICATIONS TO
COL. H. N. SCHWARZKOPF, TRENTON, N. J., or
COL. CHAS. A. LINDBERGH, HOPEWELL, N. J.

ALL COMMUNICATIONS WILL BE TREATED IN CONFIDENCE

COL. H. NORMAN SCHWARZKOPF
March 11, 1932   Supt. New Jersey State Police, Trenton, N. J.

Police chiefs in more than a thousand cities distributed posters asking for help in finding the Lindbergh baby and his kidnappers. (UPI/Corbis-Bettmann)

panions began sailing the Atlantic's waters from Block Island to Norfolk, flashing their boat's running lights and peering into the fog for a glimpse of the *Mary B. Moss*. It was nowhere to be found.

Returning one evening from an all-day search offshore, Lindy looked up to see a policeman boarding the small craft. "The baby has been found," the officer said. As the young father's face sprang alive with hope, the policeman added gently. "He is dead."

The skeletal remains of Baby Charles had been found by a New Jersey truck driver on May 12 in a heavily wooded area near the Lindbergh estate. Horrified, he notified the local police. When a state trooper arrived, the officer found the infant lying facedown, half-buried in the damp leaves and tall grass. Carefully turning the small frame he recognized the child, pale-skinned and blue-eyed, his face still partially preserved by lack of exposure to the air. A few wisps of curly yellow hair still clung to his scalp.

Within hours the police were at the door of Highfields asking to see Betty Gow. Did she have anything that matched this small scrap of material they had found nearby? Yes, she answered. The border on the fragment of fabric the police showed her matched the border on the flannel gown she had used to make Charley's nightshirt — the one he had worn the night of the kidnapping.

There could be no doubt. The dead baby found in the woods was Charles Lindbergh, Jr. Alone, while her husband was still searching the gray Atlantic, Anne Lindbergh learned that her murdered son had for months lain facedown in the woods only a few miles from home.

The work of the police now turned from searching for the baby to searching for the kidnapper. From the beginning Charles and Anne refused to believe any of their servants had been involved in the kidnapping. But now the police focused on this possibility, interviewing longtime and trusted employees of the Morrows and the Lindberghs. One of their main targets was Violet Sharpe, a maid at Next Day Hill, the estate owned by Anne's mother.

Sharpe was an attractive brunette from England. Everyone thought she would eventually marry Septimus Banks, the butler at the Morrow estate. The police wanted to know where she had been the night of the kidnapping. She had gone to the movies, she told them, but she later changed her story. She had *really* gone to a New Jersey roadhouse with a man named Ernie Brinkert, she finally admitted. Brinkert, the police discovered, was a driver for a chauffeured car service. Perhaps he had been in on the kidnapping, they speculated.

For weeks the police pressed Sharpe for information as she grew ill, lost weight, and even fainted during interviews. Finally, after being summoned for yet another round of questioning, she ran upstairs to her room at Next Day Hill, pulled a can of poison from her closet and gulped it down. Gasping, she staggered back downstairs to the pantry, where she collapsed on the floor at the feet of Septimus Banks.

Sharpe's suicide caused an uproar in the press. She had been badgered unmercifully by the police, some newspapers claimed. She had something to hide and now the secret would never be known, others reported. Members of the British government protested and called for an investigation. Mrs. Morrow told the press she believed completely in Sharpe's innocence, then sailed for Europe with Anne's brother and sister. Some people speculated that the family had something to hide.

The police meanwhile turned their attention to the ransom money. Occasionally, a bank teller or a shop clerk remembered receiving one of the ransom bills. Some remembered the person who handed the bill to them — a man with penetrating blue eyes, a pale, flat face, high cheekbones, and a triangular chin. The descriptions matched the one Dr. Condon had given of Graveyard John. And there was something else. The bills were always folded lengthwise, then double-folded again, leaving eight crease marks when they were flattened out.

The New York police had now joined in the hunt for Graveyard John. At their headquarters on Third Avenue, a map over the desk of Lieutenant James Finn was filled with an array of colored pushpins. Their positions identified places where bills from the ransom money had shown up. The pins on the wall map began to form a pattern, crowding together in a cluster in the Bronx, the northernmost borough of New York City.

Not all ransom notes showed up in the northern part of the city, though. One evening a young woman selling tickets at a movie theater in Greenwich Village was counting the receipts for the night. Her head was bent over her work when someone tossed a tightly folded bill onto the counter in front of her. She had to unfold the creased bill several times to see that it was a five-dollar federal reserve note. But it was not the bill that got her attention. It was the man buying the ticket. He was arrogant and had a strange-looking face. The next day, when the receipts from the Greenwich Village theater were deposited at a nearby bank, a young teller recognized the bill's serial number as part of the Lindbergh ransom money.

That night Lieutenant Finn went to the theater and asked the ticket seller if she could remember the man who gave her that bill the night before. She could, she told him. He had a pale complexion and hard blue, unblinking eyes. His face was almost flat, and he wore a dark hat pulled over his forehead. He sounded to Finn a lot like Graveyard John.

The police needed more, something that would lead them to John's home. They were almost sure the kidnapper had a car. Cars had license-plate numbers, and cars needed gas. The police appealed to all gas station owners in the area to be on the lookout for payment in suspicious bills.

It was September 15, 1934, when a dark blue Dodge sedan pulled into a service station on the Upper East Side of Manhattan. "Five gallons," the driver said in a heavy German accent, handing the attendant a twenty-dollar gold certificate. Thoughtfully the attendant watched as the car pulled away from the pump, then he took a pencil from his pocket and scribbled the license number on the bill's edge.

Three days later Lieutenant Finn showed up at the station. Did the attendant remember the man who gave him the bill? He did, and the description he gave fit that of Graveyard John. With mounting excitement, Finn phoned the state Bureau of Motor Vehicles. Who owned the car with that license number? The answer was Bruno Richard Hauptmann. He lived on East 222 Street in the Bronx.

The next morning when Bruno Hauptmann walked out of his small stucco house and headed toward Manhattan in his blue Dodge he was followed by several cars filled with

The lives of Charles Lindbergh and his wife Anne, both pilots during the early days of aviation, were followed closely by the press and the American public. (Library of Congress)

police officers. When Hauptmann slowed to go around a street-cleaning truck, they forced his car to the curb and pulled him from the driver's seat.

"What's this?" Hauptmann asked innocently as the men fastened handcuffs around his wrists. There was no reply as they searched his pockets and found a twenty-dollar gold note. It bore a serial number from the Lindbergh ransom money.

Anna, Hauptmann's wife, was hanging wash in the back-yard with her young son when her husband and the entourage of police arrived home. Terrified and confused, she watched as the men tore through the small apartment, turning over mattresses, rummaging through dresser drawers, and ripping apart furniture. Where was the Lindbergh ransom money? they demanded. Anna was dismayed. Hauptmann remained impassive. He knew nothing of the ransom money, he said calmly.

With Hauptmann still in handcuffs, the police hustled him into a waiting car and drove him to a police station, where they questioned him for hours. He was innocent, he claimed, and he never changed his story.

The next day the police found what they were looking for. In Hauptmann's garage a detective spotted a board nailed to the wall above a workbench. As he pulled the board off and reached into the musty hollow behind it his hand touched two bundles wrapped in newspaper. Carefully he drew the packages from their hiding place and untied them. There before him lay two stacks of federal reserve gold certificates, more than $14,000 of the Lindbergh ransom money.

The money had been given to him for safekeeping by a German friend, Hauptmann told the police. He had no idea how the friend, who had since returned to Germany and died, came to have the money, Hauptmann insisted.

The detectives were unconvinced. They had investigated Hauptmann's past and discovered he had a criminal record at home in Germany. Trained as a carpenter, Hauptmann had served in World War I, but afterward robbed the local mayor's house by climbing a ladder and entering through the second-story window. Later he held up two housewives at gunpoint. After five years in prison he stowed away on a steamship and entered the United States illegally using stolen identification. Hauptmann was formally charged with the kidnapping and death of the Lindbergh baby.

The prosecution was led by New Jersey's attorney general, David Wilentz. While he was building his case, Anna Hauptmann was trying to find a defense attorney for her husband. She had no money and little knowledge of America's legal system, so she agreed to grant exclusive interviews to a New York newspaper in exchange for their payment for a defense attorney. The paper chose Edward J. Reilly to defend Hauptmann. Known in legal circles as "Big Ed," the heavyset, flamboyant defense attorney usually appeared in court dressed in a formal morning coat, striped gray pants, and spats. He always argued his cases dramatically and admiring spectators loved to see him perform in the courtroom. When he met Hauptmann, Reilly became convinced his client was innocent.

Flemington, New Jersey, the small town where Hauptmann was tried, was not prepared for the onslaught of reporters, spectators, jurors, and celebrities who descended on the village. On January 5, 1935, the opening day of the trial, close to one hundred thousand people thronged into town elbowing each other to get into the courthouse. Others pressed into diners and cafes where menus included "Lindbergh sundaes" and "Hauptmann pudding." Crowds jostled each other to buy miniature ladders and "genuine" locks of hair from Baby Charles. The town had one hotel with only fifty rooms, and the twelve jurors doubled up to occupy six of them. Local residents took up the slack by renting rooms in their homes for exorbitant prices.

It was chic to attend the trial. Jack Benny, the comedian, was there, and so were Broadway actress Lynn Fontanne and Hollywood star Clifton Webb. A well-known novelist named Edna Ferber wrote of fashionable men in tailored topcoats and women wearing expensive minks who greeted each other exclaiming, "Isn't this divine? . . . Isn't it wonderful?" The Lindbergh kidnapping case had become the social event of the decade.

While celebrities and the simply curious gathered for the trial, Bruno Richard Hauptmann waited alone in his tiny cell in the Flemington jail. Harsh overhead lights in his cell and the adjoining hallway blazed around the clock, and his guards were ordered to remain silent in his presence. But Hauptmann seemed to take his imprisonment surprisingly well, sleeping and eating normally and occasionally singing a few bars of old German songs.

The courtroom was jammed on the first morning of the trial. Charles and Anne Lindbergh sat silently at the front of the courtroom, as the jury filed in and took their seats. Hauptmann entered, handcuffed and escorted by two state troopers.

Attorney General Wilentz opened for the prosecution, laying out for the jury what the state planned to prove during the course of the trial. Hauptmann, he said, "broke into and entered at night the Lindbergh home with the intent to commit a battery upon that child, and with the intent to steal the child. . . . As he went out that window . . . that

Bruno Hauptmann is photographed at a New York police station following his arrest for possession of the Lindbergh kidnapping ransom money. (UPI/Corbis-Bettmann)

ladder of his broke. And down he went with this child," killing the child instantly.

Wilentz painted a picture of Hauptmann's luxurious life-style following the date of the ransom payoff. "He quit his job the day he collected the $50,000, the very day . . . so that he could . . . live a life of luxury and ease." The persuasive attorney general concluded his opening speech saying, "We demand the penalty for murder in the first degree."

The jury was primed to send Hauptmann to the electric chair.

If the packed courtroom was spellbound by Wilentz, they were moved to tears by the first witness for the prosecution, Anne Morrow Lindbergh. Dressed in a fur-trimmed silk suit, the baby's mother sat pale and nervous in the witness box while Wilentz gently led her through a description of her last afternoon and evening with her son. In a soft, clear voice she told of playing with her son in the morning, putting him down for his nap, then taking a walk and stopping under the nursery window to wave at Betty Gow and the baby.

The courtroom listened to her poignant recounting of the baby's last hours alive. Wilentz held up the tattered garment found on the baby's corpse in the woods. Did she recognize it? he asked her. Yes, she replied. "It is the sleeping suit that was put on my child the night of March first." She went on to describe the rest of young Charles's outfit that night, a Doctor Denton wool sleeping suit, the one Graveyard John had sent to Dr. Condon.

When Anne finished her testimony, her husband followed her to the stand. Wilentz skillfully led Lindbergh through a series of questions to establish the state's case. Could the sound he and his wife had heard on the night of the kidnapping have been made by a breaking or falling ladder? Yes, Lindbergh replied. Then Wilentz asked him about the trip to St. Raymond's Cemetery. Had he heard anything that evening as he waited for Condon outside the cemetery walls?

"I heard very clearly a voice coming from the cemetery, to the best of my belief calling Dr. Condon," Lindbergh told the attorney.

"What were those words?" queried Wilentz.

"In a foreign accent: 'Hey, Doctor.'"

"Since that time," Wilentz asked, "have you heard the same voice?"

"Yes, I have."

Wilentz paused before posing the next question. The courtroom was very still.

"Whose voice was it, Colonel, that you heard calling 'Hey, Doctor'?"

"It was Hauptmann's voice," Lindbergh replied, looking directly at the prisoner.

Big Ed Reilly now strode forward for a cross-examination. He began by quizzing Lindbergh about the servants at Highfields. How had he hired them? Did he do background checks on them? How much did he know about them? He asked about the dog, the Lindberghs' high-strung fox terrier. He was "very nervous," Lindbergh told Reilly. Had the dog barked the night of the kidnapping? Reilly questioned. No, he had not, Lindbergh replied.

The towering defense attorney went on to establish Lindbergh's whereabouts on the night of the crime. Charles and Anne had sat in the dining room out of view of the front and back doors. The main staircase, Reilly explained, led upstairs to the bedroom and the baby's nursery.

"If the front doorway of your home was opened by someone, anyone could have gone up the stairway of your house and taken the baby out of the crib, couldn't they?" Reilly asked.

"Improbable," Lindbergh responded.

But "physically possible?" Reilly persisted.

"I don't think so," said Lindbergh. There would have been the noise of footsteps to attract their attention.

"Then, would it be possible for anyone *in* the house, *used* to the house, who *knew* the house, to take the baby out of the crib and bring it down the main stairs?" Reilly continued.

"And bring it to the door?" Lindbergh asked.

"Or bring it to a window," Reilly suggested.

It *might* have been possible, Lindbergh conceded.

"Let's take the other course, Colonel. If there was disloyalty in your home would it be possible for a person acquainted with the home to take the baby out of the crib and descend the servants' staircase and hand it to someone in the garage yard while you were dining?"

Possible, Lindbergh replied.

Reilly continued. Was the baby used to strangers? No, only friends.

"Only friends," Reilly mused thoughtfully. "You lived more or less of a reserved life, and the child was known to you, of course, and to Mrs. Lindbergh, and to Betty Gow, and to the Whateleys . . . " Wasn't it odd, Reilly implied, the baby had not cried when taken from his crib by a total stranger?

When Betty Gow took the witness stand Reilly quizzed her relentlessly about her relationship with Red Johnson. She

was the first to find out Mrs. Lindbergh would not return to
Next Day Hill the night of the kidnapping, wasn't she?

"Yes."

"Did you tell any of the help she was not coming back?"
Reilly continued.

"Probably I did."

"Did you tell Red Johnson?" Reilly asked.

"I believe so," came the answer.

And Johnson had called her about eight-thirty on the
night of the kidnapping, had he not? He had, Gow
answered.

Step by step Reilly laid out his theory for the jury. Gow
had put the baby to bed at 8:00; received a phone call from
Red Johnson at 8:30; then visited with Mrs. Whateley until
10:00, when she found the nursery empty. Wasn't the real
purpose of Johnson's phone call that night to see if the coast
was clear? Reilly thundered at Gow.

"*No*," the nursemaid screamed in reply.

The witnesses who followed, however, shored up the prosecution's case. First, there was the matter of handwriting.
The ransom note left on the nursery windowsill and those
mailed or handed to Dr. Condon were all written in a dis-
tinctive scrawl. A handwriting expert spent weeks compar-
ing the writing in the ransom notes to Hauptmann's. He
found many similarities — the Germanic spelling of words
such as "boad" for "boat," "ower" for "our," and "anyding,"
for "anything." He also pointed out that both the writer of
the ransom notes and Hauptmann had a habit of switching
"n's" and "g's." That accounted for the word "singature"

rather than "signature." Hauptmann even *pronounced* the word that way, Wilentz pointed out.

Then there was the matter of the ladder. Hauptmann had actually built the ladder himself, Wilentz told the court, and to prove his case he called Arthur Koehler to the stand. Koehler was known as the Sherlock Holmes of wood. From studying just one plank he could tell where the wood came from and what kind of saw had been used to cut it. For months he had examined the ladder used in the kidnapping and had traced most of the wood used in it to a sawmill in South Carolina. The mill had shipped the wood to a customer in New York, a lumberyard in the Bronx. Hauptmann, investigators discovered, had actually worked briefly at that same lumberyard several months before the kidnapping.

Koehler's detective work went further. One board in the ladder did not match the others. It was older wood and appeared to have been sawed off from a longer plank. Where had it come from? he wondered. The police searching Hauptmann's apartment provided Koehler with an answer when they found a loose floorboard in the attic. It had been sawed in two, and one part was missing. On the witness stand Koehler showed the jury just how the grain on the two different pieces matched. The board in the attic and the board in the kidnapping ladder had originally been one plank, he demonstrated. Furthermore, both boards were marked by identical nail holes, made with square nails.

Reilly tried to discredit the prosecution's testimony by presenting a wood expert of his own, but the damage to Hauptmann's case had been done. Both the handwriting and the wood experts presented convincing cases of the defendant's guilt.

Meanwhile during the trial Hauptmann appeared smug and arrogant. During testimony from various witnesses he shouted, "Hey, mister you are lying," and, "The old man is crazy." The courtroom was ready for fireworks when he took the stand himself. Instead they listened as Wilentz led him through a tedious accounting of his financial dealings. Since coming to the United States, Hauptmann had spent much of his time investing his money in the stock market. He kept meticulous records of all his income, including his wife's small salary. But his detailed notebooks did not include any mention of the money found hidden in his garage. Furthermore, Hauptmann had not mentioned the money to his wife, Wilentz pointed out.

"Why should I make my wife excited about it?" Hauptmann responded.

Wilentz pressed on, questioning him further about his money. An accountant walked the jury through a complicated description of Hauptmann's finances, showing him with a total of almost $50,000 in the year following Dr. Condon's payment of the ransom payment to Graveyard John. And Hauptmann had not worked since the date of the kidnapping, Wilentz pointed out. He lived lavishly, however, buying expensive items even during the Great Depression. As Wilentz attacked, Hauptmann remained calm, and even appeared amused and scornful. Enraged, Wilentz pounded away at him.

"This is funny to you, isn't it? . . . You're having fun smiling at me. . . . You think you're a big shot, bigger than everybody, don't you?" Wilentz shouted at him.

"No," Hauptmann responded contemptuously. "But I know I am innocent."

When Anna Hauptmann later took the stand Wilentz did his best to shake the alibis she provided for her husband. In the end, however, she appeared more a victim than an accomplice.

"You trusted your husband, didn't you?" defending counsel Reilly asked her gently.

"Who shouldn't trust a husband?" came her sad reply.

After thirteen days in the courtroom Wilentz and Reilly delivered their closing arguments. Reilly spoke first. "Colonel Lindbergh was stabbed in the back by the disloyalty of those who worked for him," he told the jury. Only the baby's parents, Betty Gow, and the butler and his wife, were present at Highfields on the night of the kidnapping, he pointed out.

"The person that picked that child out of that crib," Reilly continued, "knew that child and that child knew that person." He asked the jury how they could possibly believe that Hauptmann, who did not know the baby, could have entered the nursery without causing the baby to cry or the dog to bark. And how could he have backed out the second-story window, found his footing on the top rung of the ladder, which was three feet beneath the windowsill, and made his way down the rickety structure without either dropping the baby or falling? "You have a right to assume," he assured the jury, "that somebody disloyal to the colonel entered the nursery, that knew that baby."

"I believe," he said in conclusion, "this man is absolutely innocent of murder . . . and I feel sure, in closing, even Colonel Lindbergh wouldn't expect you and doesn't expect you to do anything but your duty under the law and under the evidence."

Wilentz, smartly dressed, his dark hair slicked down, took his turn painting Hauptmann as evil incarnate. The accused

Dr. John F. Condon (right) used the name "Jasfie" as he served as intermediary between the Lindberghs and the kidnapper. (AP/Wide World Photos)

had, "ice water in his veins," he proclaimed. He was "an animal lower than the lowest form in the animal kingdom, Public Enemy Number One of this world — Bruno Richard Hauptmann."

The idea of the kidnapping being an inside job was absurd, the prosecutor told the jury. Not one ransom dollar was ever traced to anybody connected with any member of the household, he reminded them. Hauptmann had murdered the baby right there in the nursery. "He crushed that child right in that room, into insensibility. He smothered and choked that child right in that room. . . . That little voice was stilled right in that room." Finally, he concluded, "You have got to find him guilty of murder in the first degree."

After instructions from the judge, the jury retired to decide Hauptmann's fate. Outside the courthouse, ten thousand people gathered to party and buy souvenirs as they waited for the verdict. As evening came and still no verdict had been returned, the carnival atmosphere turned ugly. "Kill Hauptmann! Kill Hauptmann!" the crowd chanted as they hurled rocks at the courthouse windows. At 10:45 that night, after eleven hours of deliberation, the jury filed back into the courtroom to return their verdict. Guilty, the foreman announced. Bruno Richard Hauptmann was found guilty of murder in the first degree.

Outside in the streets the crowd screamed in satisfaction. Inside, guards led Hauptmann from the courtroom. His face was devoid of emotion as he passed his wife, the reporters, the jurors, the attorneys. When he reached his cell, however, his guards said he buried his hands in his face and sobbed.

Hauptmann's execution date was set for the following month. While he waited in his cell, Anna brought their son to visit, and the couple spoke positively of plans for his appeal. Spurred on by German immigrant groups, Anna organized a Hauptmann defense fund and spoke passionately at rallies of her husband's innocence. New Jersey's Governor Harold Hoffman granted Hauptmann a stay of execution and opened his own independent investigation of the case. But the New Jersey Court of Appeals upheld the original conviction, and after more than a year of agonizing uncertainty for Hauptmann and his wife, time ran out for the German carpenter.

On April 3, 1936, a group of reporters, cameramen, and official witnesses filed through the corridors of Flemington's death house and into the execution chamber. Hauptmann entered, his head shaved and his face pale. He was accompanied by two ministers reading aloud in German from the Bible. One of the defense team read Hauptmann's final statement: "I am glad that my life in a world which has not understood me has ended . . . I am at peace with God. I repeat, I protest my innocence of the crime for which I was convicted. However, I die with no malice or hatred in my heart."

Quickly Hauptmann moved to the electric chair, sat down, and clutched its arms in a viselike grip. The executioner walked forward and fit a leather cap over the prisoner's head, then attached electrodes to each of his legs. Turning, he walked to the control panel. As two thousand volts of deadly electricity surged through Hauptmann, his body leapt, went rigid, then slumped to one side. After a moment's silence, an attending prison doctor approached the electric chair and listened for Hauptmann's heartbeat. There was none.

"This man is dead," he announced.

The vast crowd waiting outside roared its approval when the news was announced. Sitting in her nearby hotel room Anna Hauptmann covered her face with her hands and cried, "*Ach, Gott! Mein Richard!*"

Hauptmann was dead, but the effects of the kidnapping and the trial of Bruno Richard Hauptmann lasted for decades. Charles and Anne Lindbergh fled the United States to live in England in order to avoid the constant stream of threats of violence against their second son, Jon. In England the British press allowed them their privacy, and kidnapping was virtually unknown, as it had been in America until their devastating experience at Highfields. In the United States, however, kidnapping became more common, and new federal and state laws were passed to mete out punishment to the criminals involved.

Many people came to believe that Hauptmann was innocent. Some thought members of Anne Lindbergh's family had been involved and had then fled the country to avoid further investigation. Others thought Hauptmann was guilty of the crime but had been part of a larger group.

Meanwhile, Anna Hauptmann moved from the Bronx to Philadelphia with her son and, shattered by an accusation she did not understand or believe, spent the rest of her life trying to convince the world her husband died for a crime committed by others — others who went free.

4

CODE NAME, "ENORMOUS"

THE JULIUS AND ETHEL ROSENBERG
SPY TRIAL

Each day hundreds of men and women filed into a series of low wooden buildings clustered together in the isolated desert near Los Alamos, New Mexico. Their mission, known only as the Manhattan Project, was shrouded in secrecy, and only a handful of top-level scientists knew the true purpose of their work. David Greenglass, however, knew more than he was supposed to know. He was only a machinist in the tooling shop, but he knew he was helping to build an atomic bomb, which was to be the world's deadliest and most destructive weapon of war. Greenglass knew — not because he held top-secret clearance. He knew because he was a spy.

The year was 1944 and the United States was at war. America had joined Britain and Russia to help defeat Germany and Japan. Britain and the United States shared their wartime secrets. Russia, however, was not part of this inner circle. The United States and England chose not to reveal the secrets of the A-bomb to their Soviet allies. They feared that Joseph Stalin, the Communist leader who ruthlessly killed those who resisted his rule, would use the bomb to expand his power to other countries.

There were private American citizens, however, who felt Russia *should* share in these secrets. One was Julius Rosenberg, the brother-in-law of David Greenglass. Rosenberg, the American-born son of immigrant parents, grew up on New York's Lower East Side. During his boyhood years he dreamed of becoming a rabbi, but later politics and social reform became more important to him than religion. By the time he enrolled in the City College of New York (CCNY) he, like almost half of his classmates in the engineering department, joined the Young Communist League.

At CCNY Rosenberg developed a circle of friends among his classmates, many of whom shared his interest in the Communist cause. Together they marched at rallies, sold copies of the *Daily Worker,* a Communist party newspaper, and raised money for radical causes. Communism was popular among young intellectuals during the 1930s, especially among students who were horrified by the stories leaking out of Germany about Hitler's persecution of the Jews. Russia began fighting Germany in 1941 and must be sympathetic to the Jewish plight, they mistakenly assumed.

One New Year's Eve, Julius attended a union rally and noticed a short, dark-haired young woman sitting nearby. Her name was Ethel Greenglass. Ethel, like Julius, grew up on the Lower East Side. After graduating from high school she

Julius and Ethel Rosenberg were charged with conspiracy to commit espionage. Both proclaimed their innocence to their deaths. (AP/Wide World Photos)

had learned typing then took a secretarial job. She also studied singing and acting and became active in the labor union
movement. When the rally was over, the two walked home
together, talking animatedly as they strolled through the
chilly New York night.

After their fateful New Year's Eve meeting, Ethel and
Julius were always together. The two read radical news-
papers, attended union meetings, and discussed the virtues
of the communist form of government. Three months after
Julius graduated from CCNY the couple was married, with
Ethel's favorite brother, David, at her side.

In 1943 Michael, the first of their two sons, was born.
Rosenberg was working as an engineer for the United States

Army Signal Corps, where he had access to information about America's technology for tracking airplanes with radar. The Rosenbergs had little money and for social life they relied on friends they met at Communist party meetings. Ethel's brother and sister-in-law, David and Ruth Greenglass, were also dedicated party members.

Then, mysteriously, Julius and Ethel Rosenberg stopped showing up at meetings and no longer attended rallies. Perhaps, their friends thought, they had dropped out of the party. But behind the scenes Julius Rosenberg was working even more feverishly for the Communist cause. In 1943 Major Anatoli Yankolev, a Soviet agent living in New York, approached Rosenberg. Would he be willing to spy for the Soviet Union? Through his job at the Signal Corps he could pass valuable information to the Russians. And Rosenberg was still friends with former classmates from college, many of whom were now working as scientists or engineers. Perhaps Julius would recruit them, too, Yankolev suggested. Yes, Rosenberg responded. He would do both.

Spying was dangerous work, and agents took great precautions to avoid being caught. Notes were written in code. A "roof," was a front for spy operations; "neighbors" were the KGB (the Soviet intelligence agency); a "shoemaker" forged false passports. Each agent had a special code name. Julius Rosenberg's was "Liberal."

As Rosenberg began his life as a spy for the Soviets, David Greenglass enrolled in the U.S. Army. By 1943 he was the foreman in a machine shop in the lab at Los Alamos. What better contact could Rosenberg have than his own brother-in-law? Rosenberg approached Ruth, his sister-in-law and fellow Communist. The project David was working on was the most important in the world, he told her. The Russians had given it the code name "Enormous" and it would be the world's most destructive weapon of war. The Soviets were eager to have information about the atomic bomb so they could build their own. Would David be willing to collect information from the lab at Los Alamos for the Russians? Julius asked Ruth. She passed the message on to her husband when she visited him in Albuquerque. Yes, Greenglass responded. Count him in.

When Greenglass came home on furlough a few months later, he and Ruth visited the Rosenbergs. They needed to arrange for a "courier," a contact who would carry David's information from New Mexico back to a Soviet agent in New York. Sitting in his living room, Rosenberg came up with a plan. He walked into the kitchen, took a Jell-O box from the cabinet, emptied its contents, and cut one side of the cardboard carton into two jagged halves. Their contact in New Mexico would have the other half, Rosenberg told David Greenglass. Weeks later, back in Albuquerque, a man knocked on the door of the Greenglass's apartment. "I come from Julius," he said and showed Greenglass the matching half of the Jell-O box. A few days later David Greenglass presented his contact with a rough drawing of the Los Alamos lab. In exchange, he received five hundred dollars in cash.

For many years Rosenberg's spy ring went undetected. FBI agents knew people inside the United States were spying for the Soviets, but they had little information about who was involved. But the government was suspicious of Julius Rosenberg. In February 1945 he was suspended and in March fired from his job in the Signal Corps. He was a member of the Communist party, the government charged. Not so, Julius Rosenberg said, but the government thought otherwise. Not all Communists were spies, but they were among the most likely to pass secrets along to the Soviets, the government thought.

By 1945 World War II was over. The Germans surrendered first, then the Japanese, after an American B-29 bomber dropped two deadly atomic bombs, one on Hiroshima and another on Nagasaki. The bombs had been designed and built at Los Alamos, in the lab where David Greenglass had worked.

Now a new war emerged, the Cold War between the United States and its former ally, communist Russia. Eastern Europe was divided between the Communist powers and Western democratic governments. It was August 1949 when American scientists detected enormous amounts of radiation drifting from the Soviet Union. The Russians, they determined, had exploded their own atomic bomb. How had Russia, so far behind the United States and Britain in its technology, learned to build the bomb? The information must have come from inside America.

The Federal Bureau of Investigation (FBI) began tracking

down U.S. spies working for the Soviets in America. Their job was made easier when Klaus Fuchs, a British scientist, was arrested in England. Fuchs had worked on the bomb at Los Alamos and had leaked atomic secrets to the Russians. Once arrested, Fuchs began naming the names of other agents working within the U.S. He told of Harry Gold, the man who had served as his contact in New York and New Mexico. Gold was also the man with the other half of the Jell-O box, the contact for David Greenglass. When Gold was arrested in Philadelphia and sentenced to thirty years in prison, a wave of terror washed over the U.S. spy community. Three of Rosenberg's former classmates at CCNY mysteriously dropped out of sight.

David Greenglass, however, did not disappear. He was now honorably discharged from the army and living in Manhattan. Then Harry Gold identified him and his wife from a photo. In June 1950 agents from the FBI came to the Greenglass apartment and interrogated David Greenglass. They knew he was a spy, they told him. What had he done? Who else was involved? Terrified, Greenglass began to talk. Yes, he had spied for the Soviets when he was at Los Alamos. Yes, his wife was also involved. And the man who recruited them both was his brother-in-law, Julius Rosenberg.

It was early morning when FBI agents knocked on the door of the Rosenbergs' apartment. Without protest, Julius went with the agents to Foley Station for questioning, but if the FBI expected Rosenberg to give them further information on Soviet spying, they were disappointed. Everything

Greenglass accused him of was false, Rosenberg said firmly. He had never spied for the Soviets. Unconvinced, the courts let him go on $100,000 bond.

Meanwhile, David and Ruth Greenglass told prosecutors everything they knew about the Rosenbergs' activities in hopes of receiving reduced sentences for themselves. Within days police arrived at the Rosenberg apartment and hand-cuffed Julius Rosenberg in front of his two terrified sons. He was charged with conspiring to commit espionage.

Days after her husband's arrest, Ethel Rosenberg was summoned to appear before a grand jury. As she headed home from the courthouse, two FBI agents stepped forward to arrest her. Her two sons, staying with a neighbor, waited for hours, in vain, for their mother to return. Julius heard the news of his wife's arrest over the radio as he sat alone in his prison cell. It was, he told a prison guard, the darkest hour of his life.

For months, Ethel and Julius Rosenberg awaited their trial, locked in cells in separate prisons. Ethel languished in the Women's Detention Center in Greenwich Village, sobbing herself to sleep each night and suffering from migraine headaches. On mornings when the women gathered on the prison roof for exercises, she pressed her face against the chain-link fence at the edge of the building in hopes of catching a glimpse of her husband, who was housed in the men's prison nearby.

The weather was gray and overcast on March 6, 1951, the opening day of the trial. A crush of reporters and curious onlookers filed into room number 107 in the Foley Square courthouse and watched as Judge Irving R. Kaufmann began the proceedings. Irving Saypol, the government's lead prosecutor, delivered his opening statement in a flat, unemotional tone of voice. The defendants had engaged in a "deliberate, carefully planned conspiracy to deliver to the Soviet Union the information and the weapons the Soviet Union could use to destroy us." The Rosenbergs, he claimed, had made a "modern Benedict Arnold" of David Greenglass.

Saypol then called his first witness, a former college classmate of Julius's. Rosenberg had tried several times to recruit him as a spy when he was working in Washington, D.C., the witness told the court. And, he continued, he had been in a Greenwich Village apartment with an American spy for the Soviets who had photographed secret documents for delivery to Rosenberg.

Next on the witness stand was David Greenglass. Dark-haired and slightly stocky, he told the court in an even and clear voice of his early years with Julius Rosenberg. He had idolized his future brother-in-law when he was a teenager and Rosenberg was dating his older sister, Greenglass told the court. Julius had encouraged him to join the Young Communist League and later recruited him to pass secrets to the Soviets.

Greenglass then went on to tell of gathering information for Rosenberg while he worked at Los Alamos. Saypol produced a sketch, a replica of the one Greenglass had made of the "implosion lens." It illustrated, in very crude terms, the device used to detonate the atomic bomb. He had given it to

The confession of David Greenglass (right) led to the arrest of his sister and brother-in-law, Ethel and Julius Rosenberg. (Library of Congress)

Julius Rosenberg when he was home on leave in 1944, Greenglass said. It was a "pretty good description" of the bomb later dropped by the Americans on Nagasaki. Rosenberg had made a microfilm of the sketch in his apartment, Greenglass testified, then burned the original in a frying pan on the stove and disposed of the ashes by washing them down the kitchen drain. His sister, Ethel, had set up a card table in the living room and typed up the notes David had written to go with the sketch.

Greenglass also told the court of a console table in the Rosenbergs' apartment. At first glance, he told the prosecutor, the table looked quite ordinary. But Julius had shown him how it could be turned upside down to use a hidden compartment for photographing secret documents. Rosenberg had told him the Russians had given the table to him as a gift, Greenglass testified.

In his cross-examination, Emanuel (Manny) Bloch, who together with his father Alexander was the Rosenbergs' attorney, asked Greenglass about his relationship with his sister and brother-in-law.

"Do you bear any affection for your sister, Ethel?" Bloch asked.

"I do," Greenglass answered.

"You realize the possible death penalty in the event Ethel is convicted by this jury?"

"I do."

"Do you bear affection for your brother-in-law, Julius?"

"I do," answered Greenglass, but he continued to testify against them both.

As David Greenglass stepped down from the witness stand, his wife took his place. She was fashionably dressed and her dark hair was swept up in a pompadour. Confidently, she backed up her husband's testimony. She told of Ethel looking tired after allegedly staying up all night typing David's notes on the implosion lens. She gave a detailed description of Julius arranging for her and David to meet their contact in Albuquerque. She told again the story of the Jell-O box. And she testified that Julius had visited them after Gold's arrest, offering them four thousand dollars to flee the country.

When Ruth Greenglass finished her testimony, Saypol

called Harry Gold. Gold was now serving a thirty-year prison sentence for acting as the courier for Klaus Fuchs. He had also been the contact for David and Ruth Greenglass in New Mexico. He had knocked on the door of their Albuquerque apartment and said, "I come from Julius," Gold told the court. Then he had presented David with the matching portion of the Jell-O box and five hundred dollars in cash. In return, David Greenglass gave him "three or four handwritten pages plus a couple of sketches." The information had been sent to the Soviet Union and was considered "extremely excellent and very valuable," Gold said.

The next afternoon Julius Rosenberg took the stand in his own defense. Tall, thin, and pale, he wore round hornrimmed glasses and had shaved his dark mustache into a thin line. Appearing confident, he easily answered questions about his age, his marriage, his two sons, and the modest circumstances in which he and his family lived. The winter coat he wore was more than ten years old, he said, and virtually all the furniture in their fifty-one-dollar-a-month apartment was secondhand. The only time he could remember purchasing new furnishings was when he had bought a console table at Macy's, a New York department store. He had paid $21.00 for it, he said.

Rosenberg went on to deny all the charges leveled against him by David and Ruth Greenglass. Ruth Greenglass had testified that Rosenberg had enlisted his brother-in-law to spy for the Soviets, Bloch said. Had he done so?

"I did not," Rosenberg answered.

"Did you know in the middle of November 1944 where David Greenglass was stationed?"

"I did not."

"Did you know in the middle of November 1944 that there was such a project known as the Los Alamos Project?"

"I did not."

"Did you ever give Ruth Greenglass $150, for her to go out to visit her husband in New Mexico, for the purpose of trying to enlist him in espionage work?"

Again Rosenberg stood firm. "I did not."

He told the court he had never received expensive gifts from the Russians, such as a Leica camera, or an expensive Omega watch. When Bloch showed him the replica of the drawing of the implosion lens, Rosenberg said firmly, "I never saw this sketch before." Bloch then held up a photograph of Major Anatoli Yankolev, the man Gold had identified as Rosenberg's Soviet "handler" in New York. Did he recognize him? Bloch asked. "I have never seen this man in my life," Rosenberg said.

Judge Kaufman now intervened to ask Rosenberg about his political beliefs. Did he prefer the Russian form of government to that of the United States?

"I believe there are merits in both systems," Rosenberg replied. "I heartily approve our system of justice as performed in this country. . . . I am heartily in favor of our Constitution and Bill of Rights and I owe my allegiance to my country at all times."

Bloch picked up on the line of questioning.

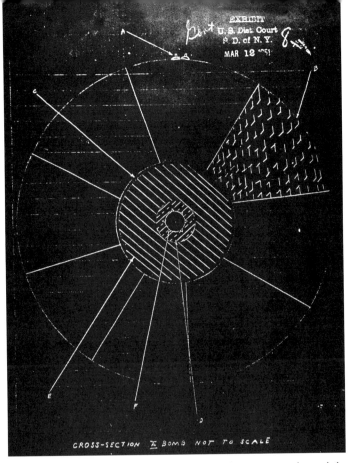

Facsimile of a simplified sketch of the atomic bomb. Attorneys charged that the sketch was developed from information gathered by David Greenglass, then passed to the Soviets by Julius Rosenberg. (UPI/Corbis-Bettmann)

"Do you owe allegiance to any other country?"

"No," replied Rosenberg, "I do not."

"Would you fight for this country?"

"Yes," Rosenberg answered.

Then Rosenberg expanded on his views about Russia. "I felt the Soviet government has improved the lot of the underdog there. . . . I felt that they contributed a major share in destroying the Hitler beast who killed six million of my coreligionists and I feel emotional about that thing."

"Do you believe in anybody committing acts of espionage against his own country?"

Rosenberg's reply was emphatic. "I do not believe that," he told the court.

It was now Irving Saypol's turn to question Julius Rosenberg. The prosecutor began his cross-examination by asking him about his feeling during World War II. Had Rosenberg believed, "if Great Britain shared in all our secrets that Russia should at the same time also share those secrets?"

"My opinion was," Rosenberg responded, "that if we had a common enemy we should get together commonly."

Saypol now led Rosenberg into dangerous waters. He asked him about his membership in the Communist party.

"I refuse to testify on the grounds it might incriminate me," Rosenberg responded. His response was based on the Fifth Amendment to the U.S. Constitution, which guarantees no person has to testify against himself.

Saypol continued to bombard Rosenberg with questions about his communist activities. Each time Rosenberg invoked the Fifth Amendment. Judge Kaufman reminded the jury they should not be influenced by Rosenberg's answer. It was his constitutional right, he told them. But the jury was left with the impression Rosenberg had something to hide.

Next Saypol zeroed in on Rosenberg's losing his job at the Navy Signal Corps.

"You were dismissed, were you not?" Saypol demanded.

"I was suspended."

"And what was the reason?"

"It was alleged that I was a member of the Communist party," Rosenberg responded.

Saypol continued, but was interrupted by Bloch.

"If Mr. Saypol wants a concession, I will concede right now that this witness was removed from Government service upon *charges* that he was a member of the Communist party."

Then came Saypol's key question.

"*Were* you a member of the Communist party?"

Again came Rosenberg's answer, "I refuse to answer on the grounds it might incriminate me."

Then Saypol asked him why he had not told the government he suspected David Greenglass of spying.

"Well, when a member of the family is in trouble, Mr. Saypol, you are not interested in sinking him," answered Rosenberg.

When Rosenberg stepped down from the witness box it was his wife's turn to testify. If the courtroom were to pick someone they thought was a spy, they scarcely would have chosen Ethel Rosenberg. She sat looking prim and composed as Alexander Bloch, the father of Emanuel Bloch, led her through a series of questions portraying her as a hardworking housewife. For a few years she worked in an office job, but after she married Julius she devoted her life to cooking, cleaning, and raising her two young sons. The sons were now in a temporary shelter in the Bronx, she told the court sadly.

She backed up her husband's testimony about the console

table. He had bought it at Macy's. And yes, she typed things from time to time on an old secondhand typewriter.

Had she typed Julius's denial he was a member of the Communist party when he was dismissed from the Signal Corps? Judge Kaufman wanted to know.

"I refuse to answer on the grounds that this might be self-incriminating," Ethel Rosenberg responded. Judge Kaufman advised her that he was only asking about typing her husband's statement, not whether Rosenberg was a Communist. But Ethel Rosenberg did not see the distinction. Nervously she responded again using the Fifth Amendment for protection. Like her husband she gave the jury the impression of having something to hide.

Irving Saypol now stepped forward to cross-examine Ethel Rosenberg. Steadily he chipped away at her composure, asking if she had friends who were members of the Communist party. She responded with the Fifth Amendment.

The judge again told the jury, "You can't infer that the witness had admitted anything from the refusal to answer."

The prosecution's next two rebuttal witnesses did further damage to the Rosenbergs' case. The first was a woman who had helped clean the Rosenbergs' apartment. Ethel had told her the console table was a gift from a friend of Julius, the maid testified. It had not come from Macy's. Next a photographer testified the Rosenbergs had come to his studio for passport photos shortly before their arrest. The jury was left with the impression the couple had planned to flee the country. And their credibility about the console table had been destroyed. Irving Saypol knew it and rested the case for the government.

The defense then made its closing summation and plea to the jury. The jury must not convict the Rosenbergs because they might be Communists, the younger Bloch said. "That is not the crime." There was not, he continued, "one piece of documentary evidence in this case to tie the Rosenbergs up with this conspiracy." The case had really been one "of the Greenglasses against the Rosenbergs."

There was no word in the English language to describe a character like David Greenglass, Bloch said. "But one thing I think you do know, that any man who will testify against his own blood and flesh, his own sister, is repulsive, is revolting, who violates every code that any civilization has ever lived by. He is the lowest of the lowest animals." Greenglass had turned government witness to save his own skin, he told the jury.

And Julius Rosenberg. Was he a high-rolling spy? No. He lived modestly. His wife cleaned and scrubbed. Look at his "client's innocent face," he instructed the jury, pointing to Ethel Rosenberg. Compare her with "Ruthie Greenglass, who came here all dolled up, arrogant, smart, cute, eager-beaver, like a phonograph record." And Gold. Gold, too, was a self-confessed spy. In closing Bloch appealed to the jury to at least save Ethel, the mother of two young children. But do not, he told them, "decide this case with your hearts. Decide it with your minds. Show the world that in America a man can get a fair trial."

Now Irving Saypol approached the jury. "Imagine a

wheel," he said. "In the center of the wheel, Rosenberg, reaching out like the tentacles of an octopus. . . . all the tentacles going to the one center, solely for the one object: the benefit of Soviet Russia."

Rosenberg and his friends had passed valuable information to the Russians, information that now lay "far away on the other side of the ocean behind the Iron Curtain," Saypol told the jury. The Rosenbergs had added "the supreme touch to their betrayal of this country by lying . . . to deceive you, to lie their way out of what they did." Ethel, he reminded them, typed up the description of the atomic bomb for delivery to the Soviet Union, "just as she had on countless other occasions sat at that typewriter and struck the keys, blow by blow, against her own country in the interests of the Soviets." He asked the jury to find the defendants guilty. "No defendants," he concluded, "ever stood before the bar of American justice less deserving of sympathy than these." The fate of Julius and Ethel Rosenberg now rested in the hands of the jury.

It was eleven the next morning when Ethel and Julius Rosenberg were called back into the courtroom. "How say you?" the clerk asked the jury. The courtroom was silent as the jury foreman rose to his feet. Both defendants are found guilty as charged, he announced solemnly.

Ethel and Julius sat shaken and stunned as Judge Kaufman thanked the jury. "My own opinion is that your verdict is a correct verdict," he said. The Rosenbergs, now convicted spies, retired to their cells to await sentencing.

When they returned to the courtroom a few days later,

the couple stood solemnly before Judge Kaufman's bench holding hands in spite of the manacles clamped on their wrists. Kaufman began to speak. Espionage is "sordid, dirty work," he said, involving the "betrayal of one's own country . . . I consider your crime worse than murder."

As Kaufman spoke, the bells of St. Andrew's, a nearby Catholic church, began tolling their noontime peals. The judge's voice was hoarse with emotion as he spoke over their clanging. "Love for their cause," he said to the court, "dominated their lives — it was even greater than their love for their children." He had struggled with his decision regarding their sentence, going to the synagogue to pray for guidance. But, he concluded, "It is not in my power, Julius and Ethel Rosenberg, to forgive you. Only the Lord can find mercy for what you have done . . . you are hereby sentenced to the punishment of death." Devastated, the Rosenbergs and defending attorney Manny Bloch left the courtroom.

Throughout the country, newspapers and radio heralded the announcement. Those convinced of the couple's treachery were jubilant. There were thousands of others, however, who were outraged at what they saw as an unfair trial, inadequate proof of guilt, and sentencing to death the mother of two young children. Klaus Fuchs, tried and convicted in a British court on charges more serious than the Rosenbergs', was sentenced to only 13 years in prison. David Greenglass, for cooperating with the government in convicting the Rosenbergs, was sentenced to 15 years in prison. His wife, Ruth, was never charged and went free.

While the Blochs prepared an appeal for a retrial, Ethel

Rosenberg was transferred to Death Row at Sing Sing prison in upstate New York. She was the only woman there awaiting execution. Manny Bloch visited her in prison, bringing her books, musical scores, and news of her two sons. As the months turned into a year and then two, Emanuel Bloch and his father led the Rosenberg case through a maze of legal maneuvers designed to save their clients from the electric chair. Each time the Rosenbergs came alive with hope. They would, they believed, be returned to their home and their sons and lead normal lives.

Meanwhile, Julius Rosenberg, too, was transferred to Death Row in Sing Sing. He and Ethel were now across the hall from each other. But locked in solitary confinement and unable to see each other, they might still have been hundreds of miles apart. Later they were allowed weekly meetings, but they were required to wear handcuffs.

Emanuel Bloch had, along with his other duties, become the unofficial guardian of the Rosenberg boys. Twice a month he drove them north from New York City to visit their parents at Sing Sing. The reunions were particularly painful for Michael, who was old enough to understand that his parents would probably be executed soon. His younger brother was excited to see his parents and happy to explore the prison.

Outside the gray walls of Sing Sing, support for the Rosenbergs was growing. Huge groups of demonstrators gathered in New York, Paris, Hong Kong, and Rome to protest the couple's execution. Supporters all across America went door-to-door with petitions demanding their release.

Benefit concerts were held to raise money for a support fund for the Rosenberg sons. Actors, writers, rabbis, and ministers publicly announced their support for the Rosenbergs. Pope Pius XII personally appealed to the United States to grant clemency. So, too, did Albert Einstein, the renowned scientist. Buoyed by the show of support, Julius and Ethel exchanged letters expressing their belief they would be saved.

Emanuel Bloch was devoting all his time and energy to appeals for the Rosenbergs, but all his efforts so far had been in vain. The date for their execution had been set. Then, only hours before the established time, two new attorneys came forward with an intriguing legal argument to present

Throughout the trial and the appeals process Emanuel Bloch, lead defense attorney for the Rosenbergs, arranged for visits to prison of the couple's two sons, Michael (left) and Robert. (UPI/Corbis-Bettmann)

to the Supreme Court. The Rosenbergs had been tried under the Espionage Act of 1917, which allowed the judge to provide the sentencing. However, Congress had since passed the Atomic Secrets Act. It provided that if a person were found guilty of passing secrets to a foreign power, the jury, not the judge, would pass sentence. The sentence for the Rosenbergs had been illegal, the two lawyers claimed.

The Supreme Court had already adjourned for its summer recess and only one justice was left in Washington. William O. Douglas considered the attorneys' argument and called the other eight justices back from their vacations to hear the case. In the meantime, the Court would grant a stay of execution while the justices conferred.

The Rosenbergs and the Blochs were ecstatic. Surely the Court would decide in their favor. Outside the white marble court building in Washington Emanuel Bloch and a large group of supporters waited in nervous anticipation. In upstate New York Ethel and Julius Rosenberg were filled with hope as they awaited word in Sing Sing prison.

Hours later the nine Supreme Court judges emerged from their chambers. They had studied the case, they announced, and found that the new law would not apply. The trial, the decision, and the sentence were all valid. On hearing the news Manny Bloch collapsed in tears.

There was, however, one more course of action. Bloch would appeal directly to President Eisenhower for clemency. Ethel Rosenberg had written a moving letter to the president. It was the last hope for the Rosenbergs, who were scheduled for execution at 8:00 that evening. They were to go to their deaths shortly after the Jewish Sabbath began. Bloch personally delivered Ethel's letter to the White House gate. Then he waited. When no word came, he phoned the White House from a nearby hotel. President Eisenhower had read the letter, he was told. He would not grant clemency. The execution would go forward.

Within seconds, Manny Bloch was on the phone to Sing Sing. He wanted one last word with Julius and Ethel Rosenberg. No, the warden told him. There was no time. The execution had been moved up an hour so it would not take place on the Jewish Sabbath. Bloch dissolved into uncontrollable tears. "Tell them I did my best," he sobbed into the phone. "Tell them I will take care of their children. Tell them I loved them. . . ." Gently his friends took the phone from his hand and led him to a nearby chair.

A few minutes later Julius Rosenberg, pale and trembling, was executed in the electric chair at Sing Sing. Then came Ethel Rosenberg. Calmly and quietly, she walked into the death chamber accompanied by the matron who had been her friend and companion during her long stay in prison. Gently Ethel Rosenberg kissed her on the cheek, then shook hands with another attendant. She sat in the electric chair and helped the executioner prepare her for death. The first violent charge of electricity that tore through her body did not kill her, and it took a second one before the prison doctor announced, "This woman is dead."

In New York City, Michael Rosenberg sat watching a Yankees' baseball game on television. As he watched, an announcer interrupted the game to announce the Rosenberg

A parade of mourners follows the hearse carrying the bodies of Julius and Ethel Rosenberg through the streets of Brooklyn. (UPI/Corbis-Bettmann)

executions. Sobbing, the young boy curled into a chair in the corner, left alone to mourn the death of his parents.

Years later, in 1996, a tall, white-haired Russian arrived in New York City on a flight from Moscow. At age eighty-two Alexander Feklisov had decided to come forward with his story. He had last seen Julius Rosenberg on a hot summer evening in 1946. The FBI was closing ranks on the Soviet spies in the United States and Feklisov, an agent for the KGB, had been told by his government to return to Moscow. He and Julius ate together at a Hungarian restaurant, then walked along the Hudson River watching the lights on the boats as they passed in the night. Feklisov gave Julius instructions on how he should contact his Soviet "handlers" once the FBI scare was over and gave him one thousand dollars in cash to cover emergencies. The two men, who had become close friends during their time working as spies for the Soviets, embraced in a final farewell.

Julius Rosenberg was a "hero" and a "great sympathizer of the Soviet Union," who had come to Russia's aid during its hour of need, Feklisov told U.S. reporters. He had met with Rosenberg at least fifty times between 1943 and 1946. Julius had helped set up an industrial spy ring that passed top-secret information on U.S. radar and military electronics to the Russians. It had been valuable material, Feklisov said, but it did not contain any atomic secrets. The secret of the bomb had not come from Rosenberg, he said. Klaus Fuchs and other scientists at Los Alamos had been responsible for that.

"Julius was a true revolutionary," Feklisov said of his old friend, "who was willing to sacrifice himself for his beliefs." Ethel, however, had never spied for the Soviets, even though she probably knew of her husband's work.

The story Feklisov told coincided with new information made public by the U.S. government. In 1996, the FBI held a press conference revealing the contents of files containing secret Russian code messages sent to spies in the United States during the 1940s and 1950s. The name of Julius Rosenberg had appeared frequently. He had clearly been an agent for the KGB. Ethel Rosenberg's name appeared only once, identified simply as Julius's wife and a member of the Communist party.

The release of the FBI files and the story told by Feklisov

put to rest a long-running argument about the innocence of Julius Rosenberg. Even those who had long argued that Julius and Ethel Rosenberg had been wrongfully sent to their deaths in a wave of anti-communist hysteria now admitted that Julius had been a spy for the Russians. The larger question now was that of the sentence. Should he have been executed or simply served a prison term? And many Americans are still haunted by the death of Ethel Rosenberg, whose greatest crime appears to have been her complete and unquestioning devotion to her husband.

5

CRAVING LIGHT

BROWN V. BOARD OF EDUCATION
OF TOPEKA

It was 1892 and Homer Adolph Plessy, a light-skinned black man, stepped into a New Orleans railroad station and bought a ticket for a trip from New Orleans to Covington, Louisiana. Then he boarded the train and took a seat in the first-class coach. Within minutes, the conductor told him to move. This car was reserved for whites only, the conductor told him. Plessy belonged in the car marked COLORED ONLY, according to law. Plessy refused to move, he was arrested, and he sued the state of Louisiana.

Plessy believed he had the same rights as any citizen of the United States. After all, the Civil War had been fought to end slavery, and the Fourteenth Amendment to the Constitution assured all citizens equal protection of the laws. But the state ruled against Plessy and so did the Supreme Court, the highest court in America. The Fourteenth Amendment assured "absolute equality of the two races before the law," the justices said, "but . . . it could not have been intended to abolish distinctions based upon color, or to enforce . . . social . . . equality."

Only one judge, Justice John Marshall Harlan, disagreed with the ruling. "Our Constitution is color-blind," he wrote in a dissenting opinion. "The thin disguise of 'equal' accommodations . . . will not mislead anyone, nor atone for the wrong this day done."

Still, segregation of the races was constitutional, the Court announced. It added, however, the state had to provide "separate but equal" facilities for both races. "Separate but equal" became the law of the land.

Fifty-five years later, Barbara Johns, a junior at the all-black Robert R. Moton High School in Prince Edward County, Virginia, stood before an assembly of students and teachers. She and her classmates had seen and heard about the attractive, well-equipped white school in their county and they knew theirs was anything but equal. Moton High, a collection of tar paper shacks, held twice the number of students it was built for and was heated only with stoves. There were no lockers, no cafeteria, no gymnasium, and inadequate toilets. The school buses were hand-me-downs from the white school. Moton students were not offered as many courses as students at white schools, and teachers received less pay.

Members of the school board said they had plans to improve Moton, maybe even build a new school. Months passed, but nothing happened. And, judging from past experiences, nothing would.

We should go on strike, Barbara Johns announced to the school. If we stop attending classes, the country will notice, and the school board will be forced to provide a better school for the black students. Then she took an even bolder step. She wrote to the NAACP, the National Association for the Advancement of Colored People, and asked for help. Before long, lawyers for the group had visited Prince Edward County, surveyed the situation, and filed suit against the state. The only solution to the problem of unequal schools was to end segregation, they stated. The public schools should be integrated.

That same year, in a run-down neighborhood in Topeka, Kansas, every weekday morning seven-year-old Linda Brown opened the door of the stone house where she and her family lived and began her long trek to school. Classes did not begin until 9:00, but she had to leave home by 7:40 to be there on time. First she threaded her way through the busy switchyard of the Rock Island Railway, dodging the huge locomotives that steamed their way along the tracks. Then she waited on a street corner for the school bus that drove her to Monroe Elementary School, almost five miles further on. Monroe was not the closest elementary school to Linda's home. There was one only seven blocks away. But the Sumner School was for white children only, and Linda was black.

In September 1951, Linda's father, Oliver Brown, took her by the hand and together the two walked a few short blocks through a pleasant well-kept neighborhood. Then they climbed the steps of the Sumner School and headed

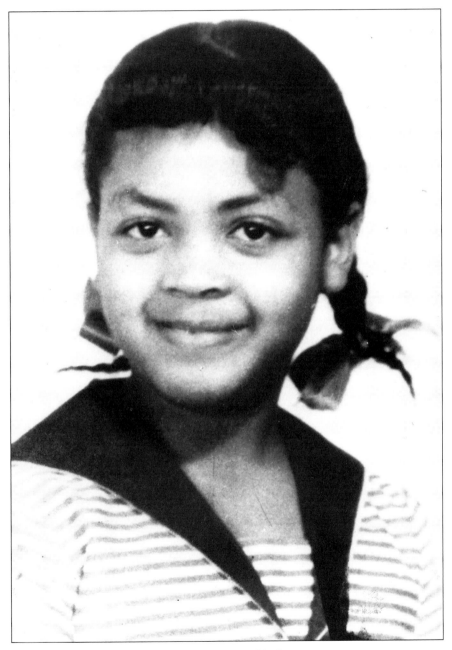

Nine-year-old Linda Brown. (AP/Wide World Photos)

down the corridor to the principal's office. He was here to enroll his daughter in school, Mr. Brown said. She was too little to make the long journey to and from the Monroe School each day. Not possible, he was told. The elementary schools in Topeka were segregated by law.

Oliver Brown was a religious, mild-mannered man, but even young Linda could see how upset he was. When the NAACP offered its help in filing a lawsuit against the Topeka Board of Education, Brown agreed. He was not the only one to do so. Other black parents were enraged that their children had to travel such long distances to all-black schools, while there were schools for white children only much closer.

Halfway across the country in New York City, the attorneys for the NAACP's Legal Defense Fund were having a busy year. They had traveled to Virginia to push for school integration in Prince Edward County, but the judges there had ruled that while schools for blacks must be made equal immediately, segregation itself did "no hurt or harm to either race." All over the country blacks were pleading with local courts to allow their children to be educated with whites. Surely, one of the cases would end up in the Supreme Court and challenge the concept of "separate but equal." *Brown* v. *Board of Education of Topeka* seemed a likely candidate. So during the third week of June, two of the NAACP's Legal Defense Fund's top lawyers, one white and one black, boarded a plane bound for Topeka to argue for school integration. The case would become one of the most controversial ones in American history.

The trial was held in Topeka's federal district court before a panel of three judges. The first witness called to the stand was Oliver Brown. Brown was no fighter, just a quiet, hard-working welder in a railroad shop. He was also a part-time minister, but nothing in his life had prepared him for presenting his case before the three solemn judges now sitting before him in the formal marble courtroom. His voice was so soft the judges had to ask him to speak up. Flustered, he began to tell the story of Linda's long journey to and from school each day. The school was 15 — no, 21 — blocks from home, he said haltingly. She had to walk through the dangerous railroad switchyard. Then she waited for the school bus, which was often late.

"Many times," Brown told the judges, "she had to wait through the cold, the rain and the snow until the bus got there." If the bus *was* on time she then had to wait outside the school for a half hour before it opened. Wasn't there a school closer to their home? the NAACP lawyer asked. Yes, Brown responded. The white school was only seven blocks away.

Other witnesses followed, each telling their own experience of seeing their children leave home in the morning to make an unnecessarily long trip to an all-black school. The final witness, Silas Hardrick Fleming, recounted his story then said he wanted to tell the court why he had gotten into the suit "whole and soul body."

"All right," said the lead judge. "Go ahead."

"Well," the witness said, " . . . it wasn't to cast any insinuations that our teachers are not capable of teaching our children because they are . . . extremely intelligent and are capable of teaching . . . white kids or black kids. But my point was that . . . the entire colored race is craving light, and the only way to reach the light is to start our children together in their infancy and they come up together."

The man's heartfelt words expressed the feelings of many other black parents. When their children were denied a chance to learn in the same schools with white children, they received an unspoken message that they were inferior. With their next witnesses, the lawyers for the NAACP set out to reinforce that idea. A professor of education at a Kansas university told the court that the black children's curriculum was limited as long as they were not allowed to attend school with white children. Whites, after all, represented 90 percent of the nation's society, he pointed out, and the black children must live in that society. "The Topeka curriculum or any school curriculum cannot be equal under segregation," the witness said.

How could that be? the attorney for the state asked. If black children learned they were equal with whites in school, how could they then possibly adjust to finding out later they could not eat at restaurants or go to hotels reserved for whites only? Wouldn't that just make their sense of inferiority even greater when they discovered that? The attorney's question was based on the widespread belief at the time that segregation in all public places would continue forever.

Another witness, Horace B. English, a psychology professor from Ohio State University, answered questions about his studies of learning patterns. Was there any difference between the learning ability of whites and blacks? Certainly not, the professor responded. But, he added, " . . . if we din it into a person that he is incapable of learning, then he is less likely to be able to learn. . . . Legal segregation definitely depresses the Negro's expectancy and is therefore prejudicial to his learning."

Another witness told the court that legal segregation leaves both whites and blacks with the impression that blacks are an inferior group. "A sense of inferiority must always affect one's motivation for learning," she concluded.

The judges hearing *Brown* v. *Board of Education of Topeka* chose to ignore the testimony in deciding the case. Segregation was not the question, they said. The question was whether black students received "equal" facilities. The state had proven the school structures *were* equal. There was, of course, the matter of the distance the children had to travel to school. But, the attorneys for the board of education had pointed out, black children were provided with school buses, while white students were not. Consequently, they concluded, "there was no willful, intentional or substantial discrimination."

The Plessy decision allowing "separate but equal" facilities had never been overruled, the judges wrote. That was a job for the Supreme Court. Until Plessy was overruled the elementary schools of Topeka would remain segregated.

The court's ruling meant Linda Brown and other young black children in Topeka would continue their long journeys to and from school. But the panel of judges had opened the door for appealing the case to a higher court. Attached to their written opinion was a section called Findings of Fact, which said that segregation retarded the educational development of black children and deprived them of benefits they would receive at integrated schools.

With this in hand, the NAACP began an appeal to the Supreme Court. And, along with it, they would ask for rulings in similar cases from Virginia, South Carolina, Delaware, and Washington, D.C. The time had come, they had decided, to end segregation.

Leading the charge at the NAACP was Thurgood Marshall, a towering black attorney with a keen mind and a quick sense of humor, who headed the NAACP's Legal Defense Fund in New York. He had grown up in Baltimore, then attended Lincoln, an elite, all-black college in Pennsylvania. When he decided to enter Howard University Law School in Washington, D.C., his mother sold her engagement ring to help pay his expenses. Howard was the premier law school for blacks in the 1930s and 1940s. Under the leadership of professor Charles Houston many of the country's top civil rights lawyers received their training there. Marshall worked extra jobs to support himself and his new young wife, commuted two hours a day by train, and still managed to graduate at the top of his class. Once out of school he represented any client who needed him, many of whom did not have enough money to pay him. Before long he had won the reputation as one of the leading civil rights lawyers in the country.

It was after he became the lead lawyer for the NAACP's

Thurgood Marshall (center) and fellow attorneys, James Nabrit, Jr., (right) and George E.C. Hayes, stand on the front steps of the U.S. Supreme Court. (UPI/Corbis-Bettmann)

national headquarters in New York that Thurgood Marshall argued his first case before the Supreme Court. It involved George McLaurin, a sixty-eight-year-old African-American with a master's degree, who was refused admission to the graduate school of education doctoral program at the University of Oklahoma. When a special district court panel ruled that McLaurin should be admitted to the state-supported school, he was. But his treatment was hardly equal to that of the white students. He had to listen to lectures seated in a small hallway separated from the main classroom. He was denied access to the public reading room in the library, and had to eat his meals alone in a separate alcove in the cafeteria. Certainly he was not receiving "equal" treatment. Thurgood Marshall prepared McLaurin's case and headed for the Supreme Court. The Court agreed. McLaurin deserved equal treatment, and should not be harassed or discriminated against. But they did not rule to end segregation. Marshall, however, had lain the foundation for building the arguments in his most important case, *Brown* v. *Board of Education of Topeka.*

The lights at the NAACP headquarters in New York burned late into the nights during the summer of 1952. Inside the offices, Marshall and his associates conferred, wrote, rewrote, and conferred some more as they prepared their briefs for the Supreme Court. Phones rang ceaselessly, and mimeograph machines cranked out letters urgently requesting donations to help pay for the work involved in the case.

Finally, the attorneys refined their basic argument for the Supreme Court. Segregation of the races in public schools violated the "equal protection" provisions of the Fourteenth Amendment. The Court should overturn the decision handed down decades earlier in *Plessy* v. *Ferguson.* It was time for the public schools of America to be integrated.

There was one aspect of the case, however, where the NAACP lawyers did not agree. What should they do with the testimony regarding the psychological effects of segregation? In one of the cases being appealed, Kenneth B. Clark, then a professor of sociology at City College of New York, told a lower court about an unusual study he had conducted. In it, a group of young children, both black and white, were presented with two dolls. One doll was black. The other was white. Which one did they think was the prettiest? Which one did they want to be like? In every case, the majority of the children of both races chose the white doll. Having been forced to attend separate schools had given black children a sense of inferiority and damaged their self-esteem, Clark contended.

Thurgood Marshall had originally objected to using Clark as a witness. Dolls? Ridiculous, he thought. But Clark's testimony had made a point. Now, preparing their argument for the country's highest court, Clark wrote a brief outlining the damaging psychological effects of segregating black children from whites. There was no mention, however, of the dolls.

As the date for the trial approached Thurgood Marshall grew more and more exhausted. He had spent all his adult life defending unpopular causes. He had worked tirelessly preparing briefs and arguing cases before hostile lawyers and judges. When he tried cases in southern states, he was not allowed to eat in restaurants serving whites and the hotels he stayed in were for blacks only. Always Marshall swallowed his resentment and played by the local rules. Why alienate the people he would meet in the courtroom more than he needed to? he reasoned. He wanted to win his cases, not prove he was a rebel. There was no money in the work he did. His reward when he won a case was the satisfaction of knowing he had helped open doors for black Americans living in a closed society.

Ten days before *Brown* v. *Board of Education of Topeka* was to be argued before the Supreme Court, Marshall traveled to Washington, D.C. He wanted time to unwind and put the finishing touches on his arguments for the case. Marshall checked into the Statler Hilton, one of the city's few first-class hotels that only recently had begun accommodating both blacks and whites. His idea of unwinding did not include long hours of rest. Instead, he recharged his batteries by staying up late into the night, refining his strategy for the upcoming case, laughing and arguing with his fellow attorneys.

In a nearby hotel, John Davis, the lead attorney for the opposing side, gathered his forces to discuss the upcoming case. Davis was in his eighties and was known as one of the country's most skillful and articulate lawyers. During his career as a Wall Street attorney he had argued 67 cases representing the government before the Supreme Court and had won 48 of those. He was respected, self-confident, and sure his arguments against school integration were sound enough to win him another victory in the Supreme Court.

On Capitol Hill in the paneled chambers of the Supreme Court the nation's highest justices pored over previous court decisions regarding segregation. Separation of blacks and whites had been the way of the land for centuries. There was scarcely a person in the entire United States who did not feel strongly about the possibility of school integration — some for, more against. The nine judges at work in their chambers knew the decision they would hand down in *Brown* v. *Board of Education of Topeka* could change the lives of more than twelve million schoolchildren throughout the nation. It was one of the most important decisions in the history of the Court.

Leading the Court was a new chief justice, Earl Warren. No one was sure what to expect from Warren. He had been a prosecutor for 13 years and had been an honest and even-handed attorney general of California. As governor of the state he supported legislation to help the poor and elderly. On the other hand, he was appointed by Dwight D. Eisenhower, the Republican president who had little commitment to civil rights. Within days of his confirmation, however, Warren had won over the other justices on the Court. He moved from office to office listening carefully to each of them, weighing their opinions and striving to bring the members to agreement on their thoughts.

On the morning of Monday, December 7, 1953, hundreds of people filed into the marble corridors of the Supreme Court building. As they entered they passed under the inscription chiseled into the marble above the building's stately doorway: EQUAL JUSTICE UNDER LAW, it read. The trial that began shortly after noon in the Court's main chamber would determine if those words would be honored.

The trial lasted three days. The first lawyer for the NAACP rose to his feet and addressed the justices seated behind the dark mahogany bench. The group included some of the most brilliant men ever to serve on the Supreme Court, and it was his job to convince them that segregation was unconstitutional. The authors of the Fourteenth Amendment had

119

a "broad purpose" in mind when they drafted it, he told the Court. But was the amendment written to apply to public schools, the justices wanted to know. There was nothing in the amendment that said it was *not* intended to include schools, Thurgood Marshall contended.

John Davis, representing the opposition, disagreed. Dressed formally in a cutaway suit, he was at his most eloquent. Their predecessors on the Supreme Court had ruled seven times that "separate but equal" was constitutional, he told the judges. And, he continued, if the schools were desegregated, in some areas blacks would outnumber whites in

Chief Justice Warren, credited with guiding the members of the Supreme Court to a unanimous decision that found segregation of schools unconstitutional. (Corbis)

the classroom. "Would that make the children any happier?" he questioned.

Davis had tears in his eyes as he addressed the court. The states could and would "produce equality for all of its children of whatever race and color," he reasoned. The Supreme Court should not serve "as a glorified board of education." That role, he concluded, belonged to the states.

Another of the defending attorneys proclaimed that "with the help and the sympathy and the love and respect of the white people of the South, the colored man has risen . . . to a place of eminence and respect throughout this nation." The segregated school system "has served him well."

Thurgood Marshall was having none of it. The blacks had never agreed to segregated schools, he said. The idea was forced on them by the white community. The South had perpetuated segregation because "they got together and decided it is best for the races to be separated," he said.

"I got the feeling on hearing the discussion yesterday," he told the Court, "that when you put a white child in a school with a whole lot of colored children, the child would fall apart or something. Everybody knows that is not true. Those same kids in Virginia and South Carolina — and I have seen them do it — they play in the streets together, they play on their farms together, they go down the road together, they separate to go to school, they come out of school and play ball together. They have to be separated in school."

There was no basis for the separation, Marshall argued. If the Court allowed segregation to continue it would be a clear message to the country that "for some reason Negroes are inferior to all other human beings."

Marshall was followed by an attorney from the U.S. Department of Justice. When the Fourteenth Amendment was adopted, public schools were not common in the United States, for either black or white children. But, the attorney said, once a state decided to offer free public schooling, "it must do it equally. . . . It is the position of the Department of Justice that segregation in public schools cannot be maintained under the Fourteenth Amendment," the young government attorney told the Court.

The judges had listened thoughtfully to three days of arguments both for and against ending segregation. It was now time for them to retire and consider their opinion. Marshall, Davis, and the other lawyers packed their briefcases and left the courtroom. Neither side could tell how the Court might rule. Throughout the hearing, the justices mostly had remained silent and without expression. There was more agreement, however, than anyone suspected.

Once alone in their conference room Chief Justice Warren led the other eight justices through the details of the case. *Plessy* v. *Ferguson* and the concept of separate but equal had been decided almost one hundred years earlier, he pointed out. Times had changed. And certainly, most of the public schools for blacks were not equal to those for white students. And he was convinced segregation was based on a belief that blacks were in some way inferior. The law, he said, "cannot, in this day and age, set them apart."

Warren knew the personalities and the opinions of the

other justices on the Court. William O. Douglas and Hugo Black, both appointed to the Court by Franklin Roosevelt, were known for supporting the causes of the poor and the powerless. They would vote with Warren. Felix Frankfurter, a brilliant former law professor and legal historian, wanted an end to segregation, but wanted to make sure the Constitution could support the move. Four justices were still uncertain. One remained adamantly opposed to desegregation.

For months the justices thought, conferred, lunched together, examined the law and their consciences, and put their thoughts on paper. Their decision would affect every citizen in the country, and Warren wanted the Court's opinion to be unanimous. They needed time to arrive at a wise decision. By spring all but one of the justices agreed. Stanley Reed, the lone holdout, feared that desegregation would cause a backlash that would undo recent advances in race relations. However, when Warren presented the justices with a written opinion in mid-May, Reed, along with the other eight members of the Court, approved the momentous decision.

Two days later Chief Justice Warren read the decision in Court. "Today," Warren read, "education is perhaps the most important function of state and local governments. . . . It is the very foundation of good citizenship. . . . Does segregation of children in public schools solely on the basis of race . . . deprive the children of the minority group of equal educational opportunities? . . . We believe it does."

Warren's clear bass voice was the only sound in the hushed

courtroom. "Segregation of white and colored children in public schools has a detrimental effect upon the colored children. The impact is greater when it has the sanction of law, for the policy of separating the races is usually interpreted as denoting the inferiority of the Negro group. A sense of inferiority affects the motivation of the child to learn. Segregation with the sanction of the law, therefore, has a tendency to retard the educational and mental development of Negro children and to deprive them of some of the benefits they would receive in a racially integrated school."

Then came the concluding statement. The Negro children who had been denied access to white schools had been "deprived of equal protection of the laws guaranteed by the Fourteenth Amendment. . . . In the field of public education the doctrine of 'separate but equal' has no place." It was the view of the Court, Warren concluded, "that the Constitution prohibits the states from maintaining racially segregated public schools."

Reporters flocked to nearby phones to announce the news to their editors. The country had walked the long road from "separate but equal" to a new day of integration. Thurgood Marshall had won his most important case, and much of the nation shared in his enthusiasm for the outcome. The Court, they felt, had acted in the best tradition of America's democratic principles. But there was the question of how the schools should be integrated. Schools would have to hire new teachers, provide transportation, and in some cases build new buildings.

The Court had anticipated the uproar its decision might

Black students leave classes protected by the National Guard during the first weeks of integration at Little Rock's Central High School. (UPI/Corbis-Bettmann)

cause in some areas of the country. There would be a second deliberation by the Court — *Brown II* some called it — to determine the best way to proceed with integration. When they met again, the justices announced that desegregation must proceed "with all deliberate speed." The courts would oversee the period of transition, they added.

Some states, however, refused to make any move toward integration. In 1957 Arkansas governor Orval Faubus called in members of the National Guard when several black children tried to attend a previously all-white school in Little Rock. Day after day the children were taunted and reviled by white parents who lined the walk to the school's front entry. Day after day the children were turned away. Finally, President Eisenhower sent five hundred paratroopers to enforce the new court order. Five years later, President John Kennedy sent three thousand troops to Mississippi to protect the rights of a student denied admission to the University of Mississippi. The following year, Governor George Wallace stood before the entrance of the University of Alabama to prevent black students from enrolling. Again, national troops were sent to escort the students safely to their classes.

In other parts of the country, however, integration went forward with little notice. And as school integration became more commonplace, other sectors of public life were desegregated. Congress passed the Civil Rights Act of 1964 and the Voting Rights Act of 1965. No one, no matter what color their skin, could be denied access to restaurants, hotels, movies, or public transportation.

Brown v. *Board of Education of Topeka* was only one step down the long and continuing road to a truly integrated society. There remained more to be done. Still, if Homer Plessy boarded a train today, he would settle into his seat surrounded by passengers of many races, the result of a court system that promises — and sometimes delivers — equal justice under the law for all.

6

COVER-UP

THE WATERGATE TRIALS

The carpeted halls of the Watergate apartment and office complex were quiet in the early morning hours of June 17, 1972. Washington, D.C., was asleep, and the watchman for the luxurious building thought he had an uneventful night before him.

Then, about two A.M., he discovered something strange. The lock on the door to one of the building's offices had been taped back, as if someone wanted to be able to enter it without being noticed. Minutes later, the watchman and three plainclothes policemen swung open the door and turned on the lights. At first everything appeared normal. Then a man reluctantly crawled out from under a desk. Then another. And then a third. In all, five men appeared from their hiding places, wearing suits and looking more embarrassed than scared or threatening.

The police surveyed them suspiciously. They did not look

like ordinary thieves. And what were they doing here? The office was the national headquarters for the Democratic National Committee, and there was little of obvious value to be taken — only some file cabinets, a few phones, and papers and memos lying on desktops. It did not look like a serious burglary. But there was something odd about it, and when the five men were charged and booked at a downtown police station, their arrests began a chain of events that shook the nation.

The break-in at the Watergate was hardly big news the next morning. There were more important stories on the pages of newspapers across the country. The United States was embroiled in an unpopular war in Vietnam, and television and news reports focused on the most recent "body count" of American soldiers killed and on the antiwar protests at home. Thousands of college students marched in demonstrations on campuses and through the streets of U.S. cities. "Hell no, we won't go," they chanted as they taunted police and publicly burned their draft cards.

At the White House, President Richard Nixon was deeply disturbed by the protests. They were overshadowing the more positive aspects of his administration, he complained to his aides. But the demonstrations continued to capture headlines.

Then there was the matter of the "leaks" to the press. In June 1971, major newspapers across the country had published the Pentagon Papers, government documents showing Nixon secretly had ordered bombings in Vietnam. The documents were leaked by Daniel Ellsburg, a researcher from California who had worked on a government report on Vietnam. Ellsberg opposed the war and had copied the documents and given them to reporters at the *New York Times* and the *Washington Post.*

The government sued Ellsberg for breach of national security, but the judge dismissed the case on a technicality. The government also sued the *New York Times* for publishing top secret documents. The information could endanger the lives of soldiers in Vietnam, the government argued. The Supreme Court saw the case differently, however, and ruled in favor of the *Times.*

Nixon was enraged. He wanted the demonstrations and the leaks stopped, he told his advisors. Nixon's advisors knew their boss well. The president had loyal supporters in the White House and within the Republican party. But, perhaps because of what he considered his humble upbringing, he never felt confident about his achievements. He continued to feel others were more privileged. He needed complete approval, and his top advisors in the White House provided that for him.

At the top of Nixon's chain of command in the White House was H.R. Haldeman, Nixon's chief of staff. He was Nixon's closest confidant, and Nixon trusted him thoroughly. In return, Haldeman did whatever he thought was necessary to protect the president and assure his reelection. John Ehrlichman, an attorney from the West Coast, served as the president's domestic affairs advisor and was equally devoted to protecting his boss's reputation. Another of Nixon's top advisors was John Dean, chief legal counsel to the president.

A bright young attorney, Dean had shown himself to be an ardent Nixon loyalist. A few blocks away from the White House John Mitchell, another avid Nixon supporter, headed up the Justice Department. As attorney general of the United States, Mitchell was the chief law enforcement officer of the land.

Word of Nixon's desire to stop the leaks, and gather information about his opponents, trickled down through the ranks of the White House staff. Nixon's top officials took his mandate seriously. On the other hand, none of them wanted to actually do any dirty work themselves. They needed someone with experience in such matters. The name of Howard Hunt came up. Hunt, a former White House

John Ehrlichman (left) and H.R. Haldeman served as President Richard Nixon's top advisors in the White House. (National Archives)

employee, had once worked for the Central Intelligence Agency (CIA). When Hunt learned of Nixon's desire for political spying, he recruited Gordon Liddy, who had also worked there. Liddy loved cloak-and-dagger operations and was eager to join the operation.

Within weeks, Liddy was on the payroll at the Committee to Re-elect the President (CRP), dreaming up schemes for stopping the demonstrators and "gathering intelligence" for the campaign. With enthusiasm Liddy presented his ideas to John Dean and John Mitchell. Their first meeting was held in Mitchell's office. Mitchell was still attorney general of the United States, the highest law enforcement job in the country. Still, Mitchell allowed Liddy to lay out his plans for illegal "dirty tricks" within the walls of his office.

One of Liddy's plans was to discredit the personal lives of the president's critics. Daniel Ellsberg, the man who had leaked the Pentagon Papers to the press, had seen a psychiatrist in Los Angeles, Liddy discovered. Maybe they could dig up some dirt on Ellsberg by breaking into the doctor's office and searching through his files. Dean wrote a memo to John Ehrlichman outlining Liddy's plan. It came back with a go-ahead. Underneath his initial, Ehrlichman had scribbled, "if done under your assurance it will not be traceable."

With Ehrlichman's approval Hunt and Liddy traveled to Los Angeles. The two had planned a discreet entry into the office and a look into the files, but the men they hired to perform the burglary left an obvious trail of broken window glass, smashed-in file cabinets, and strewn papers. To their disappointment, they found no damaging evidence about Ellsberg. To their relief, however, the police report filed after the break-in did not trace it back to Washington.

After the Ellsberg fiasco, Liddy came up with another scheme. This one was to break into Democratic National Headquarters. Perhaps they could discover who was leaking information to the press and the Democrats. Liddy and Hunt would hire a group of Cuban refugees from Miami to actually do the work. They would call them the "plumbers," since their job was to stop the "leaks." The plumbers would break into the office, place electronic bugs on the telephones, and photograph documents from the Democrats' files.

The Watergate burglary, unlike the Los Angeles break-in, *was* traceable. When the Federal Bureau of Investigation (FBI) was called in to investigate the burglary, the agents discovered the illegal phone bugs. They were hooked up, they found, to a "listening post" in a room in the Howard Johnson motel across the street. Furthermore, two men had been in that room at the motel on the night of the break-in. The two men were Liddy and Hunt. They had hired the Watergate plumbers and supervised the break-in. One of the burglars arrested was James McCord, the security chief for the Committee to Re-elect the President. Now Ehrlichman's worst fear had come to pass. This event *was* traceable. And the trail led directly to the White House.

Inside the West Wing of the White House, Haldeman met with Nixon. The things the FBI might discover could endanger the president's chances of reelection, Haldeman warned Nixon. Voters would go to the polls in less than five months. Breaking into locked offices and invading people's privacy was not something the American public wanted to associate with their president. Nixon and his aides knew that. They needed someone in their inner circle to orchestrate a "cover-up." John Dean seemed like a logical choice.

Dean's first order of business was to make sure none of the Watergate burglars told of their links to the White House. At the U.S. district courthouse in downtown Washington, John Sirica was the judge overseeing the trial for the five burglars. Sirica thought there was more to the break-in than met the eye. He and the United States prosecutor's office were determined to find out the whole truth. The White House was just as determined to make sure they did not.

The plumbers were demanding money, Hunt told John Dean. They needed money for their families and to pay their lawyers. Where was the money to come from? John Mitchell had now left the Justice Department and was chairman of Nixon's reelection campaign. The Committee to Re-elect the President had raised millions of dollars through contributions made by loyal Nixon supporters. With Mitchell's approval, part of that money was now used for payment to the plumbers.

The FBI investigation was sure to lead to more revelations, Nixon's aides told him. Use the CIA to tell them to call it off, Nixon responded. Tell them it's a matter of national security and none of their business. But the FBI was not to be deterred. As they pressed further into the case, they were able to track checks from the CRP treasury that had been "laundered" through banks in Latin America and had come back into the United States as cash. The money was distributed, with great secrecy, to the plumbers and their families. Bundles of cash were taped under phone boxes in public phone booths, left in lockers at airports, and in mailboxes in suburban Washington.

Back at the White House Nixon remained concerned. The election was less than eight weeks away. Nixon wanted the biggest landslide in history. How was the "cover-up" coming? he asked Dean. Everything was under control, the young attorney answered. "Not a thing will come crashing down to our surprise," he reassured his boss. And nothing did come crashing down. In November 1972, Richard Nixon was reelected as president of the United States.

Nixon was nervous though. He wanted to go down in history as one of the nation's most respected presidents. Instead he found himself mired in a thicket of cover-up activities. He would have done better, he now felt, to have admitted the White House's part in the Watergate burglary early on. But by now his top aides were involved in a continuing spiral of expensive payoffs to Hunt, Liddy, and the Watergate plumbers.

The Watergate burglars had been tried and found guilty in January 1973, three months after the election. At the trial the burglars testified they had performed the break-in on instructions from Liddy. When officials from the White House and the Committee to Re-elect the President were called to testify, they denied any knowledge of the break-in.

Liddy had gone off on his own, they said. He and Hunt were, according to Nixon's press secretary, "overzealous right-wingers."

Judge Sirica postponed sentencing until March. He would give the men plenty of time to consider telling what they knew in order to get reduced sentences. Howard Hunt knew the White House would do almost anything to protect Nixon's reputation. He needed more money, a lot more, Hunt told Dean. If not, he would go to the press and tell them Ehrlichman had signed off on the break-in into Ellsburg's psychiatrist's office and knew of the Watergate break-in.

Dean asked for another meeting with the president. So far he had been able to manage the cover-up successfully, he told Nixon, but now the demands were getting out of hand. "There is a cancer growing on the presidency," Dean told Nixon in an effort to impress on the president just how serious the situation had become. It would cost a million dollars over the next three years to keep Hunt and Liddy and their cohorts silent, the counsel to the president ventured.

"You could get a million," Nixon answered. "And you can get it in cash. Better damn well get that done and do it fast." Again Dean went to Mitchell. And, again, Hunt took cash from the president's men in return for his silence.

Judge Sirica and the prosecutors were still hoping one of the convicted men would come forward with more information. Finally, James McCord, the former chief of security for the presidential campaign committee, was ready to talk.

A few days before sentencing Sirica received a letter from McCord. Perjury had been committed during the trial, the letter from McCord revealed. The defendants had been pressured to remain silent. Furthermore, "Others involved in the Watergate operation were not identified during the trial when they could have been by those testifying."

McCord's confession was the first crack in the Watergate case. But in his letter to Sirica he did not say who had lied to the court or who had pressured the burglars to remain silent. There had been a grand jury in session on the break-in case since June 1972, a few days after the Watergate burglary. Now federal prosecutors convened another grand jury to explore the possibility of a cover-up.

The Watergate affair was becoming more public by the day. Two energetic young reporters, Robert Woodward and Carl Bernstein, followed every lead in the story. Much to the White House's consternation, they reported their findings each day in *The Washington Post,* one of the country's most widely respected newspapers. Democratic members of Congress also began to push for a fuller investigation of the break-in. Sam Ervin, Jr., the white-haired senator from North Carolina, headed up a special Senate committee to investigate charges of illegal fund-raising and political spying in the Nixon administration.

The president's top aides knew someone from the White House would be summoned to testify before the Ervin committee. They began to look for a scapegoat. Go to Camp David, the rustic presidential retreat in Maryland, Nixon told

John Dean. Write a report tracing the events of the Watergate affair. It did not take the young attorney long to figure out that his superiors expected him to publicly take blame for the cover-up. Unfair, Dean thought. There were others farther up the chain of command more involved than he was.

It was at Camp David that Dean decided to desert his former boss. He would go to the special Senate committee and testify. But he would not perjure himself to save the president. He would tell the truth, not what the White House wanted or expected of him. And what he would tell the senators would lead directly to the Oval Office and Richard Nixon.

Washington Post reporters Carl Bernstein (left) and Robert Woodward pursued leads on the Watergate break-in; they each won a Pulitzer Prize for their reporting. (UPI/Corbis-Bettmann)

Nixon realized that his presidency was in serious trouble. Dean could not be relied upon, and now Haldeman, Ehrlichman, and Mitchell were all under suspicion. The president felt he must move to show the American public that he would not tolerate wrongdoing among his staff. To do so, he must fire his two longtime and trusted aides. On April 30, 1973, Haldeman received a call from the president asking that he and Ehrlichman come to the Oval Office.

"I hoped, almost prayed, I wouldn't wake up this morning," the president told the two men as they stood before him. Then he broke down and sobbed. Ironically it was Ehrlichman, who was being fired, who stepped forward and put an arm around Nixon to comfort him. Nixon's last line of defense had crumbled. Looking distraught and haggard, the president went on nationwide television that evening to announce the firings in an attempt to win support.

Nixon's troubles were far from over, however. Elliot Richardson, a highly respected attorney and politician, was America's new attorney general. Congress and the American public were crying out for a thorough investigation of the Watergate affair, so Richardson appointed a special independent prosecutor, Archibald Cox, to examine the possibility of a cover-up.

Meanwhile, the investigation in the Senate proceeded. In May 1973, John Dean, his handsome face adorned with a new pair of horn-rimmed glasses, took his seat at a table at the front of the imposing Senate hearing room. In front of him were Committee Chairman Sam Ervin, Jr., and other

Senator Sam Ervin (left) prepares to hear John Dean III (seated) testify about his knowledge of the Watergate cover-up. (AP/Wide World Photos)

senators, both Republicans and Democrats. Behind him the hearing room was packed with spectators, television cameras, and news reporters.

Methodically Dean laid out the events of the Watergate affair. He told of the meetings with Mitchell and Liddy in the attorney general's office. He told of Ehrlichman's approval of the break-in into the office of Ellsberg's psychiatrist. He told of the fear that had run through the White House staff after the Watergate break-in was discovered. Haldeman had then ordered all memos about phone bugging to be shredded, Dean testified. Even Patrick Gray, Nixon's appointee to head up the FBI, had become involved, Dean told the spellbound spectators. Gray had known of the cover-up and

139

turned his head the other way. In fact, he had taken documents from Howard Hunt's safe to his own home and burned them in his fireplace along with Christmas wrappings.

For days the hearing continued as the senators bombarded Dean with questions. For days the young attorney gave detailed answers as he recalled conversations, memos, and meetings. The president was directly involved in the Watergate cover-up, he said. When told of Hunt's demands for money, Nixon had said, "We can do that," Dean told the committee. Dean appeared convincing, but many of the senators, especially the Republicans, remained skeptical.

H.R. Haldeman also testified before the committee. He told a different story. Nixon had *not* been part of the Watergate cover-up, Haldeman insisted. It was true that the president had been told of Hunt's demands for money. And it was true that Nixon had said, "We can do that." But, Haldeman testified, the president had concluded, "it would be wrong." The senators were left wondering who was telling the truth. They needed more objective evidence linking the president with the cover-up. Within days, a new witness provided them with just that.

Alexander Butterfield did not want to testify before the Senate committee. He was not a high-level aide to the president, but he knew something he did not want to reveal. On the other hand, he did not want to commit perjury. So, when he was asked if Richard Nixon secretly recorded all conversations in the Oval Office, his response was, "I'm sorry you fellows asked me that question." Yes, he admitted there was a taping system in the White House. And, yes, the tapes were still at the White House.

The tapes must be turned over to his office, Special Prosecutor Cox insisted. They were necessary to clear up, once and for all, the mysteries surrounding the Watergate affair. No, said Nixon and his advisors. The tapes dealt with national security matters, and they would not release them. Cox issued a subpoena demanding the White House to turn over the tapes. Nixon balked.

Fire Cox, Nixon ordered Attorney General Richardson on Saturday, October 20. Richardson refused. He would resign before he would fire Cox, Richardson told the president. William Ruckleshaus, the second in command at the Justice Department, also refused to fire Cox. Finally, one of Richardson's subordinates agreed to do the job. Cox was fired and Richardson and Ruckleshaus resigned from their jobs in protest. Reporters dubbed the event the "Saturday Night Massacre." The country was without leadership at the Justice Department, but Nixon had gotten his wish. There was now no special prosecutor demanding his tapes.

The public was outraged at Nixon's refusal to turn over the White House tapes and by Cox's dismissal. Reluctantly, Nixon appointed a new special prosecutor. Nixon believed Leon Jaworski would not pursue the cover-up very vigorously. He was wrong. Jaworski, like Cox, demanded that the White House turn over the tapes. Nixon sent a few reels of tape to the special prosecutor's office.

Jaworski's staff began listening to the tapes of Nixon's conversations with his top aides. One in particular caught their interest. It was a conversation that had taken place between Nixon and Haldeman three days after the Watergate break-in had been discovered. But there were long moments of silence on the reel, five gaps in all, totaling eighteen and a half minutes. How could these gaps have occurred? Jaworski and his staff wondered. The answer, provided by a sound-recording expert, was disconcerting. Someone had deliberately erased certain parts of the tape.

The White House had a different explanation. Rose Mary Woods, the president's personal secretary, appeared at court for a hearing. She had been typing a transcript of the tapes when the phone rang. She had kept her foot on the "record" pedal while she turned to answer the call, thus erasing all the sound on the tape. Jill Volner, the young attorney questioning Woods, asked her to physically reenact exactly what she had done. Woods cheerfully twisted into a contortion that required her to turn and reach with her hand almost three feet in one direction while her foot, pointed in the other direction, barely stayed on the record pedal. She had done that *five* times by mistake? Volner asked her in disbelief. Woods stuck by her story, but no one believed it was true.

Meanwhile, the lawyers at the special prosecutor's office spent hours listening to the Oval Office conversations. Nixon's deliberate voice droned an endless litany of unpleasant verbal attacks on those who had not supported his policies. Then suddenly they heard the president of the United

States talking with Haldeman and Dean about cash payments to the Watergate burglars.

"There's a real problem in raising money," they heard John Dean say. "Mitchell has been working on raising some money."

"How much money do you need?" Nixon asked.

"I would say these people are going to cost a million dollars over the next two years," Dean responded.

"You could get a million dollars," Nixon replied. "And you could get it in cash. I know where it could be gotten."

At the Senate hearings, Haldeman had told the committee that Nixon had, indeed, said, "You could get a million dollars." But, Haldeman had added, Nixon had concluded that such payments "would be wrong." Nixon had never added that last phrase, Jaworski now learned. In fact, Nixon had never questioned whether the payoffs were illegal or even unethical.

At the U.S. district courthouse in downtown Washington, a federal grand jury continued to review material about possible perjury in the Watergate case. In March Haldeman, Ehrlichman, and Mitchell were indicted on the grounds of obstruction of justice and making false declarations. Richard M. Nixon was listed as an "unindicted co-conspirator."

The war between the White House and the special prosecutor's office was growing more heated by the day. Jaworski asked for more tapes, and Nixon refused. "Executive privilege" allowed him, as president, to keep the tapes in his own possession, he claimed. This time Jaworski subpoenaed the tapes. Again Nixon refused. Again Jaworski stood firm. Finally, Nixon appealed to the Supreme Court.

In his argument before the nine justices Jaworski asked if one person, even a president, could determine what the Constitution meant. "The president may be right in how he reads the Constitution," he summarized. "But he may also be wrong. And if he is wrong, who is there to tell him so? . . . In our view, this nation's constitutional form of government is in serious jeopardy if the president, any president, is to say that the Constitution means what he says it does, and that there is no one, not even the Supreme Court, to tell him otherwise."

The Court, in an opinion read by Chief Justice Burger, a judge appointed by Nixon, ruled that the president must turn the tapes over to the special prosecutor. Three thousand miles across the country at his West Coast retreat in San Clemente, California, Nixon flew into a rage when he learned of the Court's decision. He knew what was on the tapes. And he knew the information would end his presidency.

A number of Republicans in Congress had continued to support Nixon throughout the Watergate investigation. There was no clear indication, they claimed, that the president himself had actually participated in the cover-up. There was no "smoking gun" that showed his direct involvement, just the testimony of former aides, they said. When they heard the contents of the new tapes, however, all support faded. Shaken and enraged, they listened as they heard the unmistakable voice of their president. What they heard was a conversation between Haldeman and Nixon which had taken place six days after the Watergate break-in.

Haldeman was explaining to the president the mess created by the discovery of the Watergate break-in and the FBI's investigation. It could lead back to the White House, Haldeman said. The CIA should tell the FBI to "Stay the hell out of this business here. We don't want you to go any further on it," Haldeman advised the president.

"You call them in," Nixon told Haldeman. "Good. Good deal. Play it tough. That's the way they play it and that's the way we are going to play it." There was more on the tapes, conversations that clearly proved the president of the United States had used his power, entrusted to him by the American people, to cover up crimes committed for his own political purposes. It was obstruction of justice, and it was an impeachable crime. And the tape had provided the evidence to prove it. The next day the House Judiciary Committee passed a resolution for the impeachment of the president.

There was little left for Nixon to do but resign. On the evening of August 8, 1974, Nixon went on nationwide television. Surrounded by his family, he spoke of the accomplishments of his years in office. He did not admit guilt, nor did he apologize. He must resign, he said, because to continue the investigations would completely absorb the time and attention of both the president and the Congress when their focus should be on peace abroad and prosperity at home. The next morning Nixon held a final farewell meeting with the remaining members of his staff. Then he left

THE WHITE HOUSE

WASHINGTON

August 9, 1974

Dear Mr. Secretary:

I hereby resign the Office of President of the
United States.

Sincerely,

The Honorable Henry A. Kissinger
The Secretary of State
Washington, D. C. 20520

President Nixon's letter of resignation. (National Archives) the Oval Office for the last time, stepped outside onto the White House lawn, and boarded a military helicopter waiting to carry him on the first leg of his journey back to California. He was the only president in United States history to resign.

Gerald Ford, Nixon's vice president, had just been sworn in as the new president of the United States. Within a month, Ford issued an official pardon for Nixon, an act that made it impossible for the former president to be indicted and tried for his wrongdoing while in office. Haldeman, Ehrlichman, and others on his staff were not granted similar privileges.

On October 14, 1974, the trial for those involved in the Watergate cover-up began in United States district court in Washington, D.C. Mitchell, Haldeman, Ehrlichman, and two others were charged with conspiring to obstruct justice and lying under oath. In his opening statement for the government, assistant special prosecutor Richard Ben-Veniste told the jury the Watergate cover-up was orchestrated by "the most powerful men in the government of the United States in a conspiracy that involved the participation of even the president himself." He explained to the jury the meaning of conspiracy. It is, he told the court, "no more than an agreement among two or more persons to violate the law."

Ben-Veniste went on to outline the key events of the cover-up. Just after the Watergate break-in, Hunt put an attaché case full of bugging gear into his safe at the White House along with documents that told of the break-in plan. When Ehrlichman found out he ordered Dean to "deep-six the attaché case, to chuck the whole thing into the Potomac and to shred the documents found in the safe." Instead, the prosecutor said, Dean and Ehrlichman later decided "to turn over the most damaging material in the safe directly to FBI Director L. Patrick Gray, telling Gray, in substance, that this material should never see the light of day."

Having laid out the beginnings of the cover-up, Ben-Veniste went on to tell of cash payments made to the plumbers to buy their silence. Almost $400,000 had been paid out to the Watergate burglars as hush money, he said. They would hear testimony and taped conversations that would show how extensive the cover-up had grown, the prosecutor said.

John Ehrlichman's attorney argued President Nixon, not Ehrlichman, was responsible for the cover-up. The president had "deceived, misled, lied to and used" Ehrlichman, "to save his own neck," he said. Furthermore, John Dean was an unreliable witness. He had participated in the cover-up and he had lied about it. How could the jury believe such a witness?

The next day John Dean took the stand as the government's first witness and refuted Ehrlichman's contention. Ehrlichman, Dean testified, had told him to destroy evidence of the break-in. The attorneys representing H.R. Haldeman and John Mitchell joined in the effort to discredit Dean. Dean had gone along with Nixon and others in an effort to persuade Mitchell to take the blame for the Watergate break-in. True, Dean admitted, but he had heard Mitchell discuss other possible illegal schemes prior to the break-in.

John Neal, the lead prosecutor for the government,

questioned Mitchell about his role in planning illegal campaign activities while he was still attorney general. He
reminded him of Liddy's plan to kidnap leaders who opposed the Nixon administration, drug them, and take them
to Mexico.

"Mr. Mitchell," Neal asked, "did the Liddy plan include
kidnapping? . . . Did it include getting people without their
will and taking them across to Mexico?"

"I don't know if it was Mexico but it was segregating out
radical leaders and keeping them from the activities they
were proposing to carry on or would be carrying on in con-
nection with the Republican convention," Mitchell responded.

"Was it contemplated these radical leaders would agree to
this segregation?" Neal pressed.

"I wouldn't presume so," the former attorney general admitted.

Neal reminded Mitchell of the tape of his meeting with
Nixon when the president had told him to "stonewall" the
investigation of the Watergate cover-up. "Do you remember
him telling you to 'stonewall it'?" Neal asked Mitchell.

"I remember it very well, Mr. Neal," Mitchell responded.

"And you *have* stonewalled it, haven't you?" Neal summed
up.

H.R. Haldeman claimed that his duties as Nixon's chief of
staff had kept him so busy that he was unable to know the
details of what went on around him. When asked by Ben-
Veniste about a secret White House fund of $350,000,
Haldeman said he knew the money was going to the White

House burglars but it was used, he thought, only for "legal fees and family support," not hush money.

As the trial proceeded, Judge Sirica grappled with the issue of whether to subpoena President Nixon to testify at the trial. Nixon was seriously ill and unable to participate in the trial, his doctors said. Sirica decided to send a team of three doctors from Washington to San Clemente, California, to determine if this were true. When they returned, they reported that Nixon would not be able to participate for several months in any "activity requiring substantial mental or physical effort."

But Nixon, even though physically absent, played a key role in the trial. The most damaging testimony in the trial did not come from witnesses in the courtroom. It came from the tapes of Nixon's conversations with his aides in the Oval Office in the White House. During the trial, jurors were provided earphones so they could listen to more than twenty hours of taped conversations between Nixon and his aides.

They heard Haldeman tell the president that the FBI was discovering things about the Watergate break-in that would lead to the White House. They heard Nixon tell Haldeman to use the CIA to stop the FBI from investigating further. They heard Nixon congratulate Dean on his success with the cover-up. They heard Nixon tell Dean to come up with a story that "basically clears the president." They heard the president tell Dean to draft a statement for the Senate committee saying, "no one on the White House staff is involved" in the Watergate break-in. They heard the president

President Nixon waves farewell as he boards a helicopter on the White House lawn to return to his life as a private citizen in California. (UPI/Corbis-Bettmann)

tell Haldeman and Ehrlichman that he would give "full pardons" to Watergate participants. "They'll get off," he had told them. They heard Ehrlichman tell Nixon that Dean's testimony could lead to a resolution of impeachment, "on the ground that you committed a crime."

On November 26, 1974, the prosecution rested its case. The jurors had heard 28 witnesses, 28 White House tapes, and 29 days of testimony. John Neal gave the summation for the government.

"Justice and its pursuit is an elusive goal," he began. "Our court system is a delicate institution. It can work only if it is not impeded or tampered with and only if it gets to the facts and the evidence. Justice requires access to documentary evidence and true testimony from people with information. If people can be improperly induced to remain silent an injustice will be done in one trial, then another, and then there will be no justice for any of us."

The jury retired to deliberate on December 30. On New Year's Day, 1975, they returned with their verdict. Mitchell, Haldeman, and Ehrlichman were all found guilty. Sirica sentenced them to terms of not less than 30 months and not more than 8 years in prison. The Watergate cover-up had finally come to an end.

Twenty-five years after the Watergate break-in a group of judges, lawyers, and law students met in Washington, D.C., to reenact part of the Watergate cover-up trial. They met regularly to study trials and legal ethics, and John Dean had sent a letter responding to questions about his thoughts on his involvement in the historic event.

"To this day," Dean wrote, "I cannot tell you when I crossed the line. . . . Let me say that I would never have dreamed I would go from the White House to jail. It happened," he continued, "not because I did not know right from wrong, but because I deluded myself by rationalizing that doing wrong was justifiable for political reasons and the presidency. It was not, and if my mistakes can be a lesson for someone other than myself, the experience will not have been a waste."

7

JODIE, JOHN, AND REAGAN

THE JOHN HINCKLEY, JR., TRIAL

On March 30, 1981, outside the south entrance to the Washington Hilton Hotel, a group of curious spectators sensed someone important was arriving. They had spotted the telltale television cameras and the Secret Service agents in their dark suits. "The president," murmured someone, and the news moved through the crowd. "The president's coming."

Minutes later, a sleek limousine, flanked by a protective entourage of black jump-vans, pulled into the driveway. As the crowd pressed forward, Ronald Reagan, the recently elected president of the United States, stepped out smiling and waving, then made his way into the hotel.

Less than an hour later, after a luncheon speech to a group of union delegates, the president reemerged and headed for the waiting car. He was surrounded by police and Secret Service agents. Press reporters and bystanders jostled to get nearer. "President Reagan, President Reagan!" a voice yelled out, and Reagan turned to a cameraman eager for a face-on angle. At that instant six shots rang out, six lethal Devastator bullets designed to explode on impact, fired from a .22 caliber pistol.

With lightning speed a Secret Service agent leapt into the line of fire to protect the president. As he did so, a bullet smashed into his stomach, causing him to slump to the ground. Behind him a second agent grabbed Reagan by the shoulders and slammed him down behind the open limousine door just as a fifth projectile bounced off the bulletproof glass of the car's side window. A final shot ricocheted off the back of the car and tore into Reagan's chest, puncturing his lung and barely missing his heart. A third agent fell to the sidewalk writhing in pain from a neck wound. James Brady, the president's press secretary, lay nearby, facedown on the pavement, immobilized by a bullet lodged in his brain. As Reagan, blood draining from his body, was rushed to a nearby hospital emergency room, strong-armed agents handcuffed his assailant and shoved him into a police wagon.

The young man who had just created the scene of terror that would replay on television for days to come looked the picture of innocence. From his appearance he might have been any mother's favorite all-American son. But he was not. John Hinckley was a disturbed and lonely drifter whose wealthy parents had long ago given up on their dreams of a normal life for their youngest child. John's own dream, though, had come true. He had become famous, and every-

Jodie Foster at the 1976 Cannes Film Festival received an award for her role in Taxi Driver, *a movie that became Hinckley's obsession. (AP/Wide World Photos)*

body knew his name. Maybe now, Jodie would pay some attention to him.

The Jodie of whom Hinckley dreamed was Jodie Foster. She had starred in his favorite movie, *Taxi Driver,* a film he claimed to have seen at least 15 times. For years he had been obsessed with the thought of meeting Foster, dating her, maybe taking her home to meet his parents. When police investigators searched the hotel room where Hinckley had stayed on March 29, 1981, the night before he shot Reagan, they found a letter. Hinckley had written it just before he left for the Hilton. The letter was addressed to Foster, at that time a freshman at Yale University.

"Dear Jodie," it read. "There is a definite possibility that I will be killed in my attempt to get Reagan. . . . I will admit to you that the reason I'm going ahead with this attempt now is because I just cannot wait any longer to impress you. . . . By sacrificing my freedom and possibly my life, I hope to change your mind about me." He went on to say he hoped "this historical deed" would gain her respect and love. The letter was signed, "I love you forever, John Hinckley."

Jodie Foster was not the first of Hinckley's obsessions. As a friendless teenager living in a Dallas suburb, he was devoted to the Beatles, the British rock group. He bought all their records, memorized the lyrics to all their songs, and followed every event of their lives. He taught himself to play the guitar and dreamed of a life for himself as a famous songwriter and performer.

Hinckley was eager to impress his parents, especially his father, a successful oil executive. Hinckley's mother became her son's closest friend and supporter. He had always been shy, she remembered, but in elementary school he had made friends and played football and basketball. When he entered high school in a Dallas suburb, however, John's life became alarmingly solitary.

As others in his class played sports and began dating, John withdrew to his room at home. There he brooded, listened to Beatles records, and wrote poetry. When he graduated from high school he enrolled at Texas Tech in Lubbock,

Texas. His father wanted him to major in business. John wanted to study literature and music. In the long run the decision did not matter, since John rarely attended classes and began to move restlessly from one apartment to another. His parents had now relocated to Evergreen, Colorado, a wealthy suburb outside Denver. Feeling even more alone and still friendless, John dropped out of school altogether and began his life as a wanderer.

In 1976 Hinckley sold the car his father had bought him and used the money to move to Los Angeles. From there he wrote to his parents that he was happy for "the first time in years." He was trying to sell his songs and had been encouraged by someone at one of the big Hollywood music studios. He had met an aspiring actress, the daughter of a wealthy family, and they were spending a lot of time together, John told his parents. It sounded as if things were looking up.

But Hinckley had made up the stories about his life in California in hopes of winning his parents' approval. In reality he lived a lonely, down-and-out existence. It was in Los Angeles that he first saw *Taxi Driver* and fell in love with Jodie Foster. He began to imitate the behavior of Travis Bickel, the movie's disturbed and violent cabdriver played by Robert DeNiro. He wore army fatigue jackets, bought his first gun, and read books and magazine articles about serial killers, assassins, and stalkers.

John's first letters home from L.A. were soon followed by discouraging news. He had been robbed, he was out of money, he was in poor health, and he had broken up with his girlfriend. Now he wanted to come home. His stay with his parents in Evergreen was brief. For the first time in his life he got a job, working as a busboy in a nightclub. He was frightened of driving at night, though, so he lived in a motel across the street from his work. Hinckley did not last long at the job, and soon he left town for a round of trips between Evergreen, L.A., Dallas, and Lubbock. During a visit home, he appeared so depressed his father arranged for him to visit a psychiatrist.

John needed goals, the doctor advised, and the patient was quick to come up with one. He wanted to become a writer, Hinckley told his parents. There was a writing class offered at Yale University. He wanted to travel to New Haven and enroll. Neither his parents nor his doctor had any notion of Hinckley's ulterior motive. Unsuspectingly, his father gave his son $3,600 for tuition and travel money. John boarded a plane and landed in New Haven, but did not enroll at Yale. He began instead to haunt Jodie Foster.

He waited for her outside her classes and followed her across the well-tended quadrangles of Yale's campus as she walked to her dorm. When she did appear, however, he was suddenly too shy to speak to her. He sent her flowers. He called her twice and recorded the phone conversations to play back when he was alone. He followed her from class to class and left impassioned love letters in her dorm mailbox. But Foster and her friends avoided him. Discouraged, Hinckley called his mother. He didn't like the writing class, he lied. He didn't like New Haven. He didn't like the people here. Would she pick him up at the Denver airport?

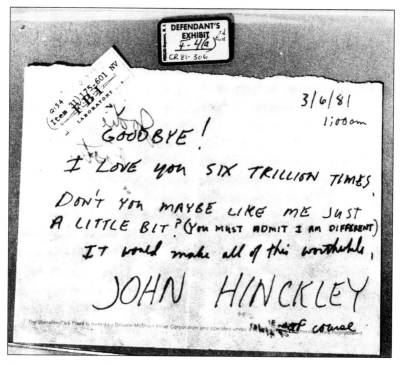

A note written by John Hinckley to Jodie Foster a few days before his attempted assassination of President Ronald Reagan. (AP/Wide World Photos)

Hinckley did fly to Colorado but first he took a train to Washington, D.C. He was devastated by Foster's rejection. He needed to make a name for himself, so she would notice him, he brooded. Assassinating a president would get attention. He began to think about shooting Jimmy Carter, then president and campaigning for reelection. Hinckley returned home and spent a few miserable days in Evergreen, then traveled to Texas and bought two more handguns. He flew to Dayton, Ohio, and attended a Carter campaign rally. Alone in the midst of hundreds of cheering people, Hinckley debated whether to make his assassination attempt.

He wasn't close enough to get a good shot, he finally decided. Besides, he had left his guns back in the hotel and he wasn't in the right mood.

The next few weeks, Hinckley made a series of plane trips crisscrossing the United States. He returned to New Haven and left more notes for Foster. He traveled to Nebraska to find a leader of the American Nazi party. He followed Carter again, this time to Nashville, where airport security arrested him for carrying handguns in his luggage. He paid a fine, relinquished his guns, and went back to New Haven. He flew to Dallas to visit his sister and buy two more guns. Then he was back in New Haven, then in Washington. Finally, exhausted and seriously depressed, he returned once again to his parents in Evergreen. When he took an overdose of tranquilizers, his parents insisted he see another psychiatrist.

Hinckley met with the psychiatrist a number of times. Their sessions together were unproductive, however. Hinckley told the doctor nothing about his fixation with Jodie Foster, his guns, his trips to New Haven, or his fascination with assassins and serial killers. And he continued to travel. He was in Washington, D.C., when he learned John Lennon, his favorite Beatle, had been shot and killed by a deranged assassin in New York. Like hundreds of other fans, Hinckley went to New York for a candlelight memorial service in Central Park.

For months Hinckley continued in his downward, nomadic spiral. Finally, following the advice of the psychiatrist, his parents told him they were no longer willing to give him money or take him in when he arrived on their doorstep. He was twenty-six years old now. He must find work and live on his own. No, his mother told him painfully when he arrived back in Denver from New York. He could not spend the night at home. She would drive him from the motel where he was staying back to the airport, however. The two drove in silence. When he turned toward her as he left the car, he said, "Well, Mom, I want to thank you for everything. I want to thank you for everything you have ever done for me." Breaking her promise to her husband and the psychiatrist, his mother opened her purse and handed her son some of her own money. Then, overwhelmed with unspoken fears for her son's life, she drove away. Alone and desolate, Hinckley flew to Hollywood, spent the night, then climbed on a bus bound for Washington. It was March 29, 1981, when he checked into the Park Central Hotel, two blocks from the White House. By the next afternoon, everyone knew his name.

President Reagan had survived his near-fatal wound, but it was a closer call than the American public knew. The press and television commentators provided reassurance by recounting Reagan's lighthearted comments in the emergency room. "Honey, I forgot to duck," he joked to his wife. Minutes later, as he was wheeled into the operating room to remove the bullet lodged in his chest, he looked up hopefully at the team of surgeons hovering above him. "Please tell me you're Republicans," he murmured as he lost consciousness. Those at the scene, however, knew Reagan was near death when he came into George Washington Hospital. He was coughing blood and gasping for breath. His blood pressure had dropped alarmingly. The surgeons did their work well, however, and within weeks, Reagan was back at work in the Oval Office.

Still, there was outrage among Americans. John Hinckley had tried to kill the president. Furthermore, he had wounded one Secret Service man and a policeman. And for months after the shooting, Jim Brady, paralyzed and unable to speak, lay in a hospital bed fighting desperately to regain some remnants of his former, active life. There was no mystery surrounding who had done the shootings. Dozens of eyewitnesses saw Hinckley crouching and shooting as the first shots rang out. The act was captured on videotape by a

Secret Service agents rush Ronald Reagan into his limo just before a bullet from Hinckley's gun seriously wounded the president. (U.S. Department of Justice)

cameraman standing in the crowd. Federal agents had immediately wrestled Hinckley to the ground and pried the gun from his hand. It seemed to most people to be a clear-cut case. Hinckley would go to trial, be found guilty, and go to prison for life, they assumed.

The case was *not* that simple, however. When Hinckley's father learned the tragic news of his son's crime, he was in Africa on a mission with a religious group. Immediately, he flew to Washington and hired a team of the city's top criminal lawyers to defend his son. Hinckley was "not guilty," his attorneys said. He was not guilty "by reason of insanity." Based on the law under which Hinckley was tried, the jury would have to answer two questions. Did Hinckley have a mental disorder that was so serious he was driven by his condition to irrationally shoot the president? And, if so, did that illness keep him from fully understanding, or "appreciating," that his act was wrong? Furthermore, the way the law was written, the burden of proof rested with the prosecution. It was not enough for the defense to convince the jury that Hinckley was insane. It was up to the government to prove beyond a reasonable doubt that Hinckley was *not* insane. The task would not be easy.

For months after his arrest, Hinckley was confined to a correctional facility in North Carolina while he waited for his trial to begin. Almost daily, Dr. Sally Johnson, a government-appointed psychiatrist, spent hours interviewing him. Hinckley liked Johnson and was flattered by her attention. He told her about his fascination with the assassins who had shot John Kennedy, Martin Luther King, Jr., and John Lennon. He recounted for her stories of his visits to New Haven and his devotion to Jodie Foster. He confided in her about his need to impress his parents. He confessed to her he was pleased seeing his name in the newspapers and hearing about himself on television. He trusted her and enjoyed having someone listen to him so attentively. A team of other government psychiatrists, led by Dr. Park Dietz, also visited him. So, too, did those hired by his lawyers, who were building a case their client was insane.

On May 3, 1982, Judge Barrington Parker entered the marble-paneled courtroom in the federal district building and called the room to order. The jurors filed in and took their seats. Across from them John Hinckley, pale and appearing disinterested, sat slumped at the counsel's table. The prosecution opened with a videotape. As the jurors and the spectators watched, they saw former President Carter shaking hands at a campaign rally in Dayton. The camera panned the crowd, then the tape slowed and stopped. There, on the screens before them, was John Hinckley, six months before he had shot Reagan.

The young man on trial in the courtroom was no innocent, mentally deranged boy, the lead prosecutor told the court. He was a dangerous "stalker and hunter" who had plotted to kill at least two American presidents.

The doctors for the defense had a different interpretation of Hinckley's psychological disorders. The defendant was delusional and obsessive, Dr. William Carpenter testified. He referred to the letter Hinckley had written to Foster just before he left his hotel for the Hilton. Most men would have given up their pursuit of a famous movie star upon rejection, he said. Hinckley, however, had persevered, believing he had a special relationship with her, in spite of evidence to the contrary. Hinckley regarded any event as relating directly to *him* personally, Carpenter testified. He thought Reagan had smiled only at him when the President entered the Hilton hotel. When he watched *Taxi Driver,* Hinckley felt abnormally connected to Jodie Foster and Travis Bickel. His mental state just before the shooting was "predominantly one of despair, depression, and a sense of the end of things," Carpenter told the court.

Was Hinckley delusional when he phoned Jodie Foster in New Haven? Roger Adelman, lead prosecutor for the prosecution, asked Carpenter in cross-examination.

"Yes," replied the doctor.

"What delusion did he have during the telephone calls?" Adelman pressed.

He felt the "only salvation that he had, the only way he could extricate himself from this life was through union with her," Carpenter explained. He felt he "had some responsibilities toward her in terms of protecting her."

But, Adelman persevered, could anyone observe these delusions?

"A delusion is a mental process," Carpenter answered. "It is not possible to have direct access to observe it. . . ."

The first rebuttal witnesses brought to the stand by the government described their encounters with Hinckley. Two maids, one from the motel where Hinckley stayed in

Dayton and another who had cleaned his room at the Park Central Hotel in Washington, told the court Hinckley had seemed like an all-American boy. Then the Secret Service agent who seized Hinckley at the time of the shooting took the stand. Hinckley had acted "calm and unemotional" and in touch with reality at the time, he told the court. An FBI agent told of carrying on a normal conversation with the defendant just after his arrest. The surgeon who had given Hinckley a medical exam the night of the shooting said Hinckley had seemed "a little anxious" and "slightly withdrawn" at the time. "But not depressed. . . . He was not out of touch with reality."

Now the government turned to its expert witnesses, Dr. Sally Johnson, Dr. Park Dietz, and other psychiatrists who had interviewed Hinckley. The defendant was, indeed, a troubled young man, Dietz, a professor at the University of Virginia, told the court. He suffered from "dysthymic disorder," or what Dietz called "sad mood" disorder. He also had a "narcissistic personality disorder," meaning he was extraordinarily self-centered and self-absorbed. Finally, he had a "schizoid personality disorder." That accounted for his lack of friends and his isolation from society. Hinckley was not psychotic, however, Dietz continued. A large percentage of the total adult population suffered from these or similar characteristics.

Hinckley was consumed with a desire for fame, Dietz went on. When he was arrested, one of his greatest concerns was whether reruns of the shooting incident would preempt the Academy Awards ceremonies scheduled to be aired that night. He was calculating in his efforts to gain publicity, Dietz said. "The setup" at the Hilton "was so unbelievably perfect," Hinckley had told Dietz. "You know, actually, I accomplished everything I was going for there. Actually, I should feel good because I accomplished everything on a grand scale."

Hinckley perked up when the next witness took the stand. He considered Dr. Johnson a friend and smiled and gave her a tiny wave as she settled into her chair to testify. Ask her if she really likes me, he urged his attorneys. Ignoring him, the lawyers turned their attention to the twenty-nine-year-old psychiatrist. She confirmed Dietz's diagnosis and recounted his absorption with assassins and fame. Many of Hinckley's behaviors were not normal, she testified. However, they did not keep Hinckley from understanding the gravity of his actions on March 30, 1981. He was capable of taking responsibility for his own behavior, she said. And, she was not convinced Hinckley had shot at Reagan just in order to impress Jodie Foster. "You're wrong!" Hinckley called out in a loud voice, interrupting the courtroom's normal formality.

Johnson continued. Hinckley had not operated on impulse, she said. In an interview with him a few days after the shooting he recalled for her what he thought just before he pulled the trigger. "I'll never have a better opportunity," he had told her. Furthermore, he had made up many of his "fantasies" with ulterior motives. He had, for instance, dreamed up his imaginary girlfriend in L.A. in order to gain his parents' approval. They would be more likely to send him money, he believed, if he were dating someone. That was manipulation, not mental illness, the doctor told the court. By the time Johnson left the stand, Hinckley was scowling and mouthing silent but obvious obscenities at her.

The defense showed the court a series of slides showing CAT scans of Hinckley's brain. The sulci, the spaces between the convolutions of the brain, were wider than normal, a psychiatrist pointed out to the court. This could indicate evidence of schizophrenia, a serious mental illness, he said.

The jury by now was mired in a confusing morass of psychiatric terms and concepts. Delusions, dysthymia, schizophrenia, sulci. Their definitions were complicated, the professional language of psychiatrists. They were led through a complicated dialogue between the attorneys and the judge as to whether Hinckley had a "substantial lack of capacity to appreciate the wrongfulness of his conduct." Just what did "appreciate" mean?

The testimony of the expert witnesses was designed to address the legal aspects of the case. But there was a more personal, emotional aspect to the proceedings in the courtroom. When the defense showed a videotape of Jodie Foster, Hinckley attentively put on his glasses, turned his chair toward the large TV screen, and smiled up at his idol's image. Foster had testified in private to avoid unwanted publicity. Hinckley, the lawyers, and the judge had been in the room with her at the time of the taping. What the jury saw was Foster telling of the harassing notes and phone calls from Hinckley. When a defense lawyer asked her to describe the nature of her relationship with Hinckley, she answered "I don't have any relationship with John Hinckley." What the courtroom did not see was what had happened at the taping. Hinckley, feeling ignored and rejected, threw a pencil at Foster in anger and threatened to kill her.

The most heartbreaking testimony for the defense came early in the trial from Hinckley's parents. His mother recalled the afternoon she drove her son to the Denver airport. "It was so hard to see John go, because I felt in my mind that once again John might be leaving and maybe he might try to take his own life. . . . We didn't say one word to each other all the way down to the airport. . . . I gave him some money of my own. . . . He looked so bad, and so sad, and so absolutely in total despair and I was frightened. . . ." When he got out of the car he thanked her, she recalled in court. "I said, 'Well, you are very welcome.' And I said it so coldly because I didn't want him to know what I was thinking."

Hinckley's mother was followed on the witness stand by her husband. He remembered meeting John at the airport when he came home one final time in March 1981. He had told his son, Jack Hinckley recounted painfully, how disappointed he was in him. "I took him to his car which was parked at the airport. It was an old car and the radiator leaked. And I put some antifreeze in it and we got the car started. And I had a couple of hundred dollars with me that I had brought from the house. And I gave that to him and I suggested that he go to the YMCA and he said, No, he didn't want to do that. And so I said, 'OK, you are on your own. Do whatever you want to.'"

The court was quiet except for the sound of the sobs coming from Hinckley's mother. "In looking back on that I'm sure that was the greatest mistake in my life. I am the cause of John's tragedy," Hinckley's father said. "We forced him out at a time that he just simply couldn't cope. I wish to God that I could trade places with him right now."

In summing up for the defense, one of Hinckley's attorneys played a tape recording Hinckley had made on a lonely and solitary New Year's Eve in 1981.

"John Lennon is dead," the jury and the gallery heard. "The world is over. Forget it . . . it's just going to be insanity, if I even make it through the first few days. . . . I still regret having to go on with 1981. . . . I don't know why people wanna live. . . . John Lennon is dead. . . . I still think — I still think about Jodie all the time. That's all I think about really. That, and John Lennon's death. They were sorta binded together.

"I hate New Haven with a mortal passion. I've been up there many times, not stalking her really, but just looking after her. . . . I was going to take her away for a while there, but I don't know. I am so sick I can't even do that. . . . It'll be total suicide city. . . . Anything I might do in 1981 would be solely for Jodie Foster's sake."

The unhappy ramblings were only part of the tape, the attorney told the court. "I think," he said, "it reflects a very disturbed state of mind, a state of mind which is totally de-

Hinckley is restrained by federal agents as presidential press secretary James Brady lies wounded on the sidewalk. (UPI/Corbis-Bettmann)

tached from reality." He then went on to catalogue the various events that had led to Hinckley's assassination attempt. John Hinckley was a seriously disturbed young man, disturbed to the point of insanity. He was incapable of controlling his actions. The government, he concluded, had failed to prove Hinckley was mentally responsible and able to conduct his life according to the law.

Adelman now rose to his feet to sum up for the prosecution. Hinckley was clearly guilty of shooting Reagan, Jim Brady, and two Secret Service agents. What they were to consider, the attorney told the jury, were the events of March 30, 1981, not the events leading up to that date. That was when the shooting occurred. And, "Who brought

171

the gun to Washington?" Adelman asked. "John Hinckley. The Devastator bullets? Who brought them to Washington? John Hinckley."

John Hinckley was a "sad, depressed person," the prosecutor continued, but he could tell right from wrong. He referred to the events leading up to the shooting as a "parade of irrelevancies." The jury was not trying Hinckley on the basis of his mental state on New Year's Eve. "I think if we tried a lot of people's mental condition on New Year's Eve, it might be similar to John Hinckley on that date. We are trying March 30, 1981," he reminded the jurors. And on March 30, 1981, Adelman asserted, John Hinckley *was* able to "appreciate the wrongfulness" of his actions. He *was* able to "conform his behavior" to follow the law. In other words, he was not insane. Concluding, the prosecutor asked the jury to find the defendant guilty.

The jury took two and a half days to return their verdict. When they did, the nation and the prosecutors were stunned. John Hinckley was "not guilty by reason of insanity." How, asked thousands of Americans, could a gunman whose very act of shooting the president was recorded on videotape be found not guilty? But the jury, burdened by the intricacies of the law and the testimony of the expert witnesses, had concluded just that.

Hinckley was sent to St. Elizabeth's Hospital in southeast Washington, D.C., a mental institution with a ward for the criminally insane. In an evaluation when he was admitted, hospital psychiatrists wrote, "Mr. Hinckley is presently a danger to himself, Jodie Foster and any third party whom he would consider incidental in his ultimate aims."

Hinckley, however, was comfortable at St. Elizabeth's. His life had structure and he was surrounded with people who paid attention to him. "I see a therapist, answer mail, play my guitar, listen to music, play pool, watch television, eat lousy food and take delicious medication," he told an interviewer for a national magazine. Sometimes patients asked for his autograph, he added. Did he enjoy the attention he was now getting? the writer asked. He'd be lying if he said he didn't, Hinckley responded.

Hinckley was annoyed, though, at not being able to talk

Hinckley protected by federal agents as he is driven from U.S. District Court. (UPI/Corbis-Bettmann)

on the phone and having his mail censored. He wanted that changed. Actually, his doctors agreed that he needed less isolation and more contact with society. Encouraged, Hinckley asked if he could take walks around the hospital grounds. The answer was yes. Next, he asked that he be allowed to spend one day a month in the city — by himself. This time the answer was a firm no.

The role of the hospital was to help Hinckley get better. He received medication and therapy. By December 1984, the staff doctors felt their patient was ready for a brief holiday visit with his parents in nearby Virginia. Hinckley rode in a car accompanied by a hospital escort. Close behind, a car full of Secret Service agents followed. They had learned of the furlough only days before and neither their agency nor the courts had been consulted. They were not happy to see Hinckley out of confinement.

A few months later the hospital again granted Hinckley permission for a holiday visit with his parents — this one for Easter. This time there would be no hospital escort with him. The prosecutors from the government refused permission for the visit. The hospital must have prior approval from the court before they granted Hinckley any kind of furlough. But Hinckley's doctors from St. Elizabeth's argued at a court hearing that their patient was much improved. He was no longer obsessed with Jodie Foster. "It is the hospital's opinion that Mr. Hinckley does not pose a danger to himself or others if granted this limited privilege."

There was, of course, the matter of the letters. "He writes letters to some of his pen pals," the doctor revealed. And just who were these pen pals? the court wanted to know. Hinckley's lawyers looked uncomfortable as the doctor answered. There was Ted Bundy, the convicted serial murderer, now serving time in a Florida prison. Hinckley had written to him expressing his sympathy for the "awful position that Bundy must be in." And there was "Squeaky" Fromme, the woman who had attempted to kill President Ford. Hinckley had also asked for the address of Charles Manson, the infamous mastermind of the slaughter of a houseful of young people in Hollywood several years earlier. Judge Parker issued an order for the patient's room to be searched. Even the hospital staff was astounded at what they found. Embarrassed, they withdrew their request for Hinckley's holiday release. Hinckley's obsession was far from over. Hidden in his room they found twenty photographs of Jodie Foster.

For years Hinckley continued to make requests for permission to leave the grounds of St. Elizabeth's. One request, made years after the shooting, was denied when the court discovered that Hinckley was obsessed with a female pharmacist at the hospital, a woman who reminded him of Jodie Foster. At each request, the courts ruled no. Hinckley remained dangerous, they felt.

As with most major trials, the Hinckley trial resulted in changes in the law. In 1984 Congress enacted a statute that, among other things, requires the defense rather than the prosecution to bear the burden of proof in an insanity case.

The case also resulted in the passage of a stricter handgun law. Hinckley left behind him a severely shattered life for

James Brady, the press secretary shot in the head at the time of the assassination attempt. Brady, with the determined support of his wife, spent years relearning how to walk, feed himself, and talk. He did so with great difficulty. He was able, however, to join his wife in campaigning for what became known as the Brady Bill, which made it more difficult to buy handguns. John Hinckley would have had a harder time assembling his arsenal of weapons had that law been in effect when he made his first trip to a Texas gun shop in 1976. Jim and Sarah Brady hoped the new law might save others from the tragedy of a random shooting. Whether John Hinckley was sane or insane remained an unsolved legal issue. The greater issue became the insanity of too many guns on the streets of America. Meanwhile, American presidents led more and more isolated lives as the Secret Service tried to protect them from the dangers posed by crazed, would-be assassins.

8

MURDER IN L.A.

THE O.J. SIMPSON TRIAL

On June 17, 1994, more than 95 million Americans sat transfixed in front of their television screens as they watched a white Ford Bronco inch its way forward on a California freeway. The scene itself was a dull one. But the voices of the news commentators told a story of fame, desperation, and flight. The driver of the vehicle was a friend of O.J. Simpson, a retired football star, sports broadcaster, and sometime actor. And Simpson was crouched in the back of the vehicle with a gun held to his own head. Simpson was a fugitive from justice. Now with the nation watching he was headed back to Los Angeles. Dozens of police were waiting for him, waiting to arrest him. They would arrest him because he was a prime suspect in a grisly double murder.

A couple out walking had found the bodies, having been led to the brutal scene by a whining, restless white Akita with blood on its paws. The dog belonged to the new owner of a stucco townhouse at 875 South Bundy Drive, one of the busier streets of Brentwood, an otherwise quiet and wealthy section of Los Angeles. The new occupants, a blond mother and her two young children, had moved there only six months earlier. Previously they had lived in the neighborhood in a palatial estate at 360 North Rockingham Avenue. The home on Rockingham belonged to O.J. Simpson. And it was Simpson's ex-wife, Nicole, the neighbors had found lying faceup in an oozing pool of blood, her throat slit with a knife.

Shortly after midnight on June 13, a Los Angeles policeman had answered a call from one of Nicole Brown Simpson's neighbors. Shining his flashlight down the dark walkway at the side of Ms. Simpson's townhouse he found two terribly mutilated bodies. One was a woman dressed in a black dress, her throat slashed almost through to her spine. The other was a young man. His neck also had been slashed and his torso and thighs were gashed with stab wounds. Both bodies lay in large pools of blood.

A dog's bloody paw prints led toward the street. Shoe prints led in the other direction, away from the bodies to a gate at the back of the property. Drops of blood ran along the left side of the shoe prints. The door to the house was ajar and inside the lights were on and music was playing. An envelope with O.J. Simpson's return address lay on the hall table. A poster of Simpson hung on the wall, along with family photos showing O.J., his wife, and their children.

Quickly the policeman realized the murdered woman outside the house was Nicole Brown Simpson. But who was the murdered man?

The officer called in to the headquarters of the Los Angeles Police Department (LAPD). Within minutes squad cars began streaming into the neighborhood. Word of the murders spread quickly as police rang doorbells asking residents what they had seen and heard. The two Simpson children, Sydney and Justin, were asleep upstairs. An officer bundled them into blankets and carried the pair to a police car, carefully avoiding the crime scene where their mother lay murdered.

Meanwhile more police continued to pour toward the Bundy Drive address. Behind the taped-off crime area, investigators made notes on what they saw. There was a black knit ski cap at the foot of the man's body. A leather right-handed glove lay near the body of Nicole Brown Simpson. Nearby was a bloodstained envelope containing a pair of woman's glasses. It was the glasses, police discovered later, that had brought the young man to the Simpson house. He was Ron Goldman, a waiter at Mezzaluna, a nearby restaurant. Nicole Brown Simpson's mother had left the glasses there earlier that evening when she, Nicole, the children, and other family members had dined there. In the simple act of returning them, Goldman had become an innocent victim in a deadly assault.

As members of the LAPD's homicide division arrived, they made a quick survey of the scene. They needed to let

O.J. Simpson know right away about the murder. They did not want him to learn of the crime through news reports or from reporters showing up on his doorstep. Four homicide detectives piled into a couple of police cars and headed to 360 North Rockingham Avenue to find O.J. Simpson. When they arrived, he was not there. He was, they discovered, halfway across the country in Chicago.

The Simpson estate in Brentwood was a sprawling timber and stone mansion surrounded by a six-foot wall. The grounds included an outdoor swimming pool, a tennis court, and a guesthouse. Simpson had grown up in San Francisco with little money and enjoyed the fortune he had earned in sports and advertising endorsements. He had become famous when he attended the University of Southern California on a football scholarship. In his senior year he won the coveted Heisman Trophy, awarded to the nation's best college football player. Then, as a highly paid running back for the Buffalo Bills, he piled up a record-breaking two thousand and eleven yards in one season before heading back to the West Coast to play for the San Francisco 49ers. Simpson became a football legend.

Those who did not know Simpson from the football field recognized him from his engaging television ads for the Hertz auto rental company. Dressed nattily in a suit and carrying a briefcase, Simpson was shown making an impressive run through a crowded airport from the Hertz counter to catch a departing plane. On screen and in much of his private life, Simpson appeared charming and easygoing.

There was another side to Simpson's life, however. His

O.J. Simpson became a national football hero when he received the Heisman Memorial Trophy in 1968. (UPI/Corbis-Bettmann)

first marriage had ended in divorce. When he met Nicole Brown, she was eighteen and he was in his thirties. They differed not only in age but in race. He was black and she was white. But the attraction was strong, and a few years later they married. They had a daughter and a son and shared interests in their children, sports, and partying with friends. Then, things began to go sour.

In the mid-1980s, Mark Fuhrman, a policeman for the Los Angeles Police Department, had gone to Simpson's Rockingham home in response to a 911 call from Nicole Brown Simpson. When he arrived, he found her outside the house. Her husband had smashed the window of her Mercedes-Benz with a baseball bat, she told Fuhrman, but she did not press charges.

A few years later, on New Year's Eve, 1989, police responded to another 911 call. The operator answering the call had first heard only silence, then the sound of a woman screaming and someone being hit. The operator traced the call and sent a squad car to 360 North Rockingham Avenue. When police arrived at the Simpson mansion, they found Nicole Brown Simpson disheveled and near hysterics, again outside the house. Her face and neck were marred with red welts and bruises. "He's going to kill me! He's going to kill me!" she wailed. Yes, she told the officers, this time she was willing to sign a police report calling for Simpson's arrest. Simpson was charged and pleaded "no contest." Suspended sentence, the judge ruled. Simpson was fined and ordered to get counseling and perform community service.

In 1993, there was another frantic call from Nicole Brown

Simpson to 911, this one from her Bundy Drive home. O.J. had shown up at her house and was "ranting and raving . . . going nuts," she told the operator in a frightened voice.

Now shortly before dawn on June 13, 1994, four homicide detectives left the Bundy house and headed to the estate on Rockingham Avenue. Philip Vannatter, the lead detective on the case, pressed the buzzer on the wall surrounding the grounds of Simpson's house. There was no answer, though there were lights on in the house and cars parked in the driveway. Vannatter tried again and again, but still no one appeared. Mark Fuhrman, the officer who had responded to one of Nicole Brown Simpson's 911 calls years earlier, was with Vannatter.

Later, people questioned why Fuhrman was at the scene since he had not been assigned to the case. Nonetheless, he wandered away from the gate and shined his flashlight on a white Ford Bronco parked at an angle at the curb on the street. He thought he saw bloodstains on the door on the driver's side, he told Vannatter, who was still trying to rouse someone inside the house. There was still no answer.

Finally, Fuhrman climbed over the wall and opened the gate from the inside. When the officers rang the bell and knocked on the door of O.J.'s house, again there was silence. Then they went around back and roused Arnelle Simpson, O.J.'s daughter by an earlier marriage, who was staying in a guest apartment at the back of the estate. Her father had left for Chicago late the night before, she told the police. Fuhrman then knocked on the door of another guest apartment, and Kato Kaelin, a young man with long blond hair, sleepily opened the door. Fuhrman shined his flashlight in Kaelin's face and began questioning him.

Kaelin lived rent-free in the little apartment behind Simpson's large house. He did not socialize much with O.J., he told Fuhrman, but the night of the murders on Bundy Drive he had gone with him to McDonald's. The two left the house about 9:00, Kaelin told Fuhrman and, later, a grand jury. They had returned about 9:40 and Kaelin went back to his apartment. About 10:45, back in the guesthouse, Kato was talking on the phone when he heard three loud thumps on his back wall. They were so loud he thought it might be an earthquake. At 11:00, he said, Simpson had knocked on his door and asked him to help carry his bags to the waiting limousine. He was headed for Chicago, Simpson told Kaelin, to play in a golf tournament the next day.

Mark Fuhrman was interested in Kaelin's story. What had caused the noise behind the guesthouse? he wondered. He walked outside, around to the dark, narrow passageway at the back of Kaelin's apartment that ran between the guesthouse and the back wall of the estate. According to what he later told a jury, in the beam of his flashlight he spied something on the ground near the air-conditioning unit at the back of Kaelin's apartment. Fuhrman looked closer. Lying on the leaf-covered path was a glove, a glove for a right hand. It had blood on it, and it looked a lot like the left-handed glove police had found on the walkway on Bundy Drive, next to Nicole Brown Simpson's dead body.

As Fuhrman talked with Kaelin, Philip Vannatter was trying to locate O.J. Simpson, who was staying in a hotel in

Chicago. Vannatter put in a call to Simpson and broke the news to him. "Oh my God, Nicole is killed?" Simpson gasped. "Oh my God, she is dead?" He would take the next flight home, he told Vannatter.

After the phone call to Simpson, Vannatter began to examine the Rockingham estate more closely. There were drops of blood in the foyer of the house, he noticed, and also a trail of drops from the front gate leading to the front door. How about the Bronco? he wondered. He wanted a closer look at that, too. Peering through the side window he saw what he thought was blood on the inside of the door on the driver's side. The police felt evidence was accumulating that pointed to O.J.'s involvement in the murders, and Vannatter wrote up an order requesting a search warrant for Simpson's Brentwood estate.

When Simpson arrived home from Chicago he went with Vannatter to police headquarters for questioning. Simpson sat in a small room with Vannatter, another officer, and a tape recorder and answered questions about his whereabouts during the last 48 hours. He'd gone to his daughter Sydney's dance recital the night before, he told them. But he had not joined Nicole and the rest of her family for dinner at the Mezzaluna restaurant afterward. Instead, he had tried to get in touch with Paula Barbieri, his girlfriend. Then he returned home and went out for a hamburger with Kato Kaelin at "eight-something, maybe." After he came home he had hurriedly packed for his late-night departure for Chicago, he said.

How about that cut on his left hand? Vannatter asked

him, pointing to a bandage on Simpson's middle finger. He'd cut it in Chicago, Simpson responded. Did he have another cut *before* he went to Chicago? Maybe a little one, Simpson said. He remembered bleeding in the house and in the Bronco before he left for the airport. But it was "no big deal," he added. The police had found blood at his house and blood in the Bronco, Vannatter told him. The discoveries raised some questions. They would have to take some blood samples from Simpson. No problem, Simpson agreed. "I know I'm the number-one target."

Even after the detectives' interview, a number of details remained murky. There were the blood tests, though. Crime experts from the LAPD ran tests on the blood samples taken from O.J. and the drops of blood found on the pathway at Nicole Brown Simpson's house. The samples matched. They ran tests on the blood on the glove Fuhrman found behind O.J.'s guesthouse. The blood belonged to three people, they concluded: Nicole Brown Simpson, Ron Goldman, and possibly O.J. Simpson. The L.A. prosecutor's office decided it was time to move.

On June 17, the district attorney's office filed charges against O.J. Simpson for the first-degree murders of Nicole Brown Simpson and Ronald Goldman. Simpson was ordered to show up for arraignment no later than eleven that morning. He would be there, Simpson's lawyer assured the court. By two o'clock that afternoon he had not appeared.

O.J. had fled in a white Ford Bronco with his friend Al Cowlings at the wheel, headed south on a California freeway. His lawyer, Robert Shapiro, went on the air and pleaded with O.J. to turn himself in. A friend read a suicide letter O.J. had left behind. His flight, he wrote in a rambling note, had nothing to do with Nicole's murder. On the contrary, he wrote: "Unlike whats been in the press, Nicole + I had a great relationship for most of our lives together. Like all long-term relationships, we had a few downs + ups."

At about six-thirty that evening a pair of motorists noticed a white Ford Bronco behind them as they headed north on the Santa Ana Freeway. They notified the police. Cowlings had heard the radio pleas for Simpson's return and had persuaded him that they should turn around. Soon an odd procession, headed by Cowlings and Simpson, led a slow parade toward Los Angeles. As squad cars followed behind, the Bronco inched northward. Spectators, aware of the event from television and radio reports, lined the highways. Supporters held signs hastily painted with SAVE THE JUICE and yelled encouragement as the car went by. Helicopters flew overhead as TV camera crews filmed the scene from above. Soon almost all of America was watching.

At 8:00 P.M. Cowlings pulled the Bronco into the driveway of Simpson's house. An hour later, Simpson gave up the gun he was holding to his temple and emerged from the Bronco. He did not resist as officers handcuffed him. Simpson was headed to jail. Inside Cowlings's Bronco police found Simpson's passport, a fake goatee and mustache, and a loaded handgun.

Marcia Clark, a dark-haired prosecutor assigned to the Simpson case, thought her job would be easy. Everything, she reasoned, including the blood tests, the glove, and Simpson's attempt to flee, pointed to his guilt. But Clark had not counted on the so-called Dream Team, the group of attorneys Simpson hired to defend him in court. Shortly after he arrived back from Chicago, Simpson called Robert Shapiro, a criminal attorney well-known in L.A. for his successful plea bargaining for celebrities in trouble with the law. Shapiro assembled other noted defense lawyers to represent O.J. There was Alan Dershowitz, a Harvard University professor of criminal law. There was F. Lee Bailey, a defense attorney who had made his name winning acquittals for his high-profile clients. Then there were four experts with special knowledge of crime scenes and DNA testing, special laboratory analyses of hair, blood, and tissue samples that could identify a person's unique genetic fingerprint. And there was Johnnie Cochran, an African-American trial lawyer famous for trying civil rights cases in California. It was an impressive defense lineup.

Nothing about the Simpson case went unnoticed. It became one of the biggest media events in America's history. The case touched on many of America's most popular interests — celebrities, sports, wealth, and race relations. The *Today* show, *Larry King Live, Oprah,* and every other television talk show in the country featured a legal expert. Radio and television stations played a tape of one of Nicole Brown Simpson's frantic calls for help to the police emergency 911 number. By the time the trial actually began, almost everyone in the country had strong opinions about the case, one way or another.

Simpson and his wife Nicole Brown Simpson at a 1993 Thanksgiving Day football game. (AP/Wide World Photos)

In a pretrial hearing Judge Kathleen Kennedy-Powell ruled on what evidence was permissible and what would be suppressed. And the public was allowed to watch the trial on television. Television cameras were new to the courtroom. Viewers saw the families of Nicole Brown Simpson and Ron Goldman. They saw O.J. Simpson's elderly mother, wheelchair-bound by arthritis, and his sister and oldest daughter. They listened to a lengthy discussion between the judge and the lawyers about how many hair samples could be taken from Simpson's head for testing. Marcia Clark's changes in hairstyle became headline news, and spectators

189

followed with fascination the details of the personal lives of Clark and Cochran.

Viewers listened as the defense argued that the early search of O.J.'s estate had been illegal. The police detectives had scaled the wall and let themselves onto the estate grounds without a proper search warrant. They had only one purpose that morning, the defense said. They wanted to find evidence linking O.J. with the crimes. The television audience watched as Philip Vannatter tried to convince the judge otherwise. He and the other detectives scaled the wall and let themselves into the grounds simply to find O.J., he testified. They were afraid O.J. himself might have been a victim of some crime. And they wanted to tell him personally of his ex-wife's murder. Most viewers were not convinced by Vannatter's story. The judge, however, ruled the evidence could be admitted at the trial.

Simpson entered his plea to the court on July 22, 1994. He looked fit and handsome as he entered the courtroom and gave the spectators in the room a thumbs-up. He was, he announced firmly, "Absolutely, one hundred percent not guilty."

Under the Constitution of the United States, any citizen accused of a crime is innocent until proven guilty. Thousands of Americans believed from the beginning that Simpson had killed Nicole Brown Simpson and Ron Goldman. Others, however, believed Simpson was innocent. And many feared that as an African-American, he would never get a fair trial in the Los Angeles area. Their beliefs were based on the reputation of the LAPD. For years, black residents in

L.A. had complained about brutal treatment from white officers on the city's police force. On March 4, 1991, that reputation spread across America when the nation watched, horrified, as the evening news replayed a videotape taken by a motorist in the early morning hours of March 3 on an L.A. freeway. It showed four L.A. policemen savagely beating a black motorist named Rodney King. The officers were brought to trial before an all-white jury and were acquitted. Riots broke out in black neighborhoods in L.A. Resentment toward the police smoldered. Many people, especially blacks, now viewed the LAPD as oppressors rather than protectors.

Judge Lance Ito was appointed to oversee the trial. In September 1994, a pool of 900 potential jurors appeared before him at the criminal court building in downtown Los Angeles. After endless questions, the pool was pared down to just over 300. Some actually seemed eager to serve in spite of the fact they would be sequestered, isolated from their families, news reports, and any contact with the outside world. Finally, 24 people were selected, 12 jurors and 12 alternates. The jury included eight women and four men. All eight women were African-American. Of the men, one was white, one was Latino, and two were of mixed race.

There were cameras everywhere on the morning of January 24, 1995. Outside the L.A. courthouse helicopters circled overhead while spectators, photographers, and reporters pressed forward to catch a glimpse of the lawyers as they entered the building. And with TV cameras allowed inside the courtroom, people throughout America watched as Judge Ito called the court to order. Christopher Darden, an

African-American lawyer from the district attorney's office, opened for the prosecution. He urged the jury to see beyond O.J. Simpson's public face. He wanted them to look at "the other side you never met before . . . the face of a batterer, a wife beater, an abuser . . . the face of Ron's and Nicole's murderer." Simpson knew he was no longer welcome in Nicole's life, Darden said. He had seen that clearly the night of his daughter's dance recital. He was not invited to join Nicole, her parents, and his own children at the Mezzaluna restaurant after the recital, Darden pointed out. "He was no longer being treated as a part of the family. . . . Nicole was getting on with her own life . . . she left him. She was no longer in his control. He could not stand to lose her," the prosecutor concluded, "and so he murdered her."

Marcia Clark followed Darden. With precision she laid out the case for the prosecution. She told of the dog barking at 10:15 and the neighbor's discovery of the murdered bodies. She told of Kato Kaelin's trip to McDonald's with Simpson. She told the jury they would hear from Allan Park, the limousine driver who had come to take Simpson to the airport shortly after the time of the murders. Simpson had not been there, she said. She showed gruesome pictures of the murder victims and talked of the blood found at the scene. The DNA tests would show the blood matched O.J. Simpson's, she assured them.

The blood on the glove found at O.J.'s house was his, she continued, along with that of the two murder victims. The hair samples found in the black knit cap at the crime scene matched those taken from O.J. She spoke of the footprints found at the murder site. They were size twelve, she told the jury, the same size as the defendant's. O.J. Simpson had killed Nicole Brown Simpson, Clark concluded. He had taken her "youth, her freedom, and . . . her very life. . . . And in that final and terrible act, Ronald Goldman, an innocent bystander, was viciously and senselessly murdered."

Johnnie Cochran opened for the defense. They were on a search for justice, he told the jurors, a search for truth. He told them of the witnesses they would hear. One had been walking along South Bundy Drive at the approximate time of the murders, he told them. She had seen four suspicious men, none of them black, with knit hats on their heads, Cochran said, but the prosecution had chosen not to

Prosecutors Marcia Clark and Christopher Darden hold a press conference after the defendant is found not guilty. (AP/Wide World Photos)

investigate her story. The prosecution also had chosen not to talk in their opening statements about Detective Mark Fuhrman, Cochran pointed out. There was a reason for that. The defense knew the reason and they would have a good deal to say about him, he promised. He touched on the matter of the evidence and the DNA tests. Those from the LAPD were not reliable, he cautioned.

The first witness called by the prosecution was the 911 operator who had taken the call from Nicole Brown Simpson on New Year's Eve, 1988. The call had come from 360 North Rockingham Avenue, she told the court, and she had dispatched the police as soon as she heard the sounds from the other end of the line. Darden played a recording of the phone call, a horrifying silence broken only by a woman's screams and the sounds of someone being hit.

Darden played a recording of another of Nicole's calls for help to 911. This call, made on October 25, 1993, had lasted 13 minutes. The courtroom was utterly still as they heard Nicole's terrified voice. "He's back. Please . . . He's O.J. Simpson. . . . Could you please send somebody over?" In the background O.J. screamed in rage as Nicole pleaded with him to leave. "I'm leaving with my two fists is when I'm leaving," he yelled in anger.

Later Denise Brown, Nicole's oldest sister, took the stand. She told of visiting Nicole and O.J. at their Rockingham house. O.J. had flown into a rage, she told the jury. He tore pictures from the wall and threw Nicole's clothes downstairs. Then he " . . . threw her out of the house."

Other prosecution witnesses told of what they had seen

and heard the evening of the murders. Officer Robert Riske of the LAPD, who had found the two murder victims, described what he had seen at the Bundy Drive house.

Johnnie Cochran cross-examined Riske about how evidence was recorded at the crime scene. What about the dish of melting ice cream that was on the back stairway at the house? Why had no photo been taken of that? Why had that not been considered evidence? He questioned him about the coroner. Why had he not arrived earlier to examine the bodies? Surely the delay made it impossible to determine the exact time of the victim's death. He questioned Nicole Brown Simpson's character and linked her again to a close friend who was a known drug user. The most damaging questioning from the defense, however, was to come later in the trial.

For weeks, the Simpson trial dragged on. Judge Ito had promised the jurors the trial would probably conclude by February 1995. But things moved slowly. With cameras in the courtroom, proceedings took on a Hollywood atmosphere. Attorneys on both sides played to the gallery. Judge Ito allowed rambling cross-examinations and sometimes reversed his decisions. Tempers flared and lawyers engaged in open arguments. Marcia Clark and Judge Ito locked horns.

The members of the jury, who spent each night isolated in a downtown L.A. hotel, were growing restless. Things picked up, however, on March 9 when Marcia Clark called Mark Fuhrman to the stand. Clark had thought Fuhrman would help convince the jury of O.J.'s guilt. He was, after all, the man who had found the now-famous bloody glove

Ron Goldman, who was murdered with Nicole Brown Simpson. (AP/Wide World Photo)

on the grounds of Simpson's estate. He was good-looking and spoke confidently. She began by asking Fuhrman about his first visit to 360 North Rockingham when he had gone there in response to a 911 call from Nicole Brown Simpson in 1985.

Clark then moved on to more dangerous territory. She knew that the defense had discovered damaging evidence about Fuhrman. If she brought it up, she reasoned, it would defuse the issue. A real-estate agent had written to Johnnie Cochran about overhearing Fuhrman talk with some friends about his work as a policeman. He had said he would like to see "all niggers gathered together and killed," the woman told Cochran. The woman's letter had been leaked to the press before the trial began and Clark now decided to tackle the issue head-on. Did that conversation ever take place? Clark asked. "No, it did not," Fuhrman answered definitively.

It was now the defense team's turn to cross-examine Fuhrman. F. Lee Bailey rose and tried to discredit the police detective. He referred to Fuhrman's racial slurs. He implied that Fuhrman had moved the left-handed glove from the Bundy Drive house to 360 North Rockingham. He asked if Fuhrman had wiped the glove in the Bronco. "No," Fuhrman responded.

Bailey now focused on the racial issue. "Do you use the word 'nigger' in describing people?" he asked Fuhrman.

"No, sir," the detective responded.

Had he used that word in the past ten years? Bailey questioned. Again, Fuhrman said he had not.

"So that anyone who comes to this court and quotes you as using that word in dealing with African-Americans would be a liar, would they not, Detective Fuhrman?" Bailey pressed.

"Yes, they would," Fuhrman answered. His answer would soon turn out to be a lie.

Marcia Clark was eager to return the jury's attention away from the racial attitude of Mark Fuhrman to the actions of O.J. Simpson on the night of the Brentwood murders. The prosecution had a convincing witness in Allan Park, the driver who had come to 360 North Rockingham to pick up Simpson on the night of June 12. Park told the court of arriving early at Simpson's house, at about 10:25. There were no lights on, and there were no cars parked in front of the house on Rockingham. Park pulled onto the side street next to the estate and rang the buzzer at the side entrance to the house. No one answered. He waited and tried again. Then again. He became worried Simpson would not catch his 11:45 plane.

About 10:50 the driver finally saw someone inside the gate, a tall black man walking from *outside* the house in through the front door. When Park buzzed again, lights went on and Simpson came to the door, claiming he had overslept. Kato Kaelin helped Simpson carry his bags to the waiting limousine and O.J. climbed in. As the driver pulled out of the driveway and onto North Rockingham, Park noticed something. A white Ford Bronco was now parked at the curb, parked at an angle as if someone had left it in a hurry.

The prosecution felt good about Park's testimony, but they were in for a hard time when Barry Scheck, a DNA expert for the defense, began his cross-examination of Dennis Fung, the forensic expert who had gathered the evidence at the crime site and at Simpson's North Rockingham home. Scheck questioned Fung extensively about every detail of his procedures. Before he was through, Fung admitted to giving different testimonies to the grand jury and at the trial. Perhaps he had actually contaminated some of the evidence,

Fung said nervously after hours of questioning. He became confused about what he did when and how he did it.

Fung, for instance, had collected a pair of dark socks at the foot of O.J. Simpson's bed the morning after the murders. In looking at them in ordinary light he had not noticed any blood on them. Nor had he mentioned any blood on them in his report. It was only weeks later that the forensic lab tested them and found blood on them — blood the lab tests showed matched Nicole Brown Simpson's.

There was also the matter of the blood on the back gate at Nicole Brown Simpson's South Bundy Drive condo. Fung had not made note of a spot of blood on the gate the morning after the murders. Three weeks later, however, he returned and found a bloodstain there. Only then had he taken a sample for testing. When the results came back, the blood sample matched that of O.J. Simpson. There was only one chance in 57 billion that it was not Simpson's. But Scheck skillfully set out to show the jury that the tests could not be trusted.

Not all of the blood collected from Simpson after his arrest could be accounted for, Scheck pointed out. When O.J. Simpson was interviewed by police the day after the murders, he willingly allowed a nurse to take approximately 8 ml of his blood for testing. Vannatter put the vial in his pocket. The testing lab was in downtown L.A., but instead of taking it directly there, Vannatter pocketed it and drove 25 miles to the Rockingham estate. It was there that he handed the sample over to Fung, who then allowed it to sit in an unairconditioned police van in the hot California sun.

Later, the forensics department of the LAPD could only account for 6.5 ml of Simpson's blood sample.

Scheck drew two damaging conclusions. First, the heat in the police van could cause the blood to break down and give inaccurate results. More seriously, since not all the blood could be accounted for, Vannatter or other members of the LAPD might have deliberately planted blood in Simpson's Bronco, on the socks, and on the left-handed glove. The prosecution had more DNA tests that showed the drops of blood next to the footprints at Bundy Drive matched O.J.'s blood sample. There was only a 1-in-170-million chance they came from someone else. But Scheck had seen the LAPD's forensic lab and called it a "cesspool of contamination." The blood test results were not reliable, he told the court. The LAPD was incompetent at best, he implied, corrupt at worst.

The prosecution had hoped to use evidence showing that the footprints found near the murdered bodies were made from shoes owned by O.J. Simpson. They were, after all, made by a size twelve shoe, the same size Simpson wore. The prints appeared to come from Bruno Magli shoes, expensive Italian footwear, but the prosecution was not able to prove Simpson owned such a pair of shoes.

What came next in the courtroom became the most memorable moment of the trial, when O.J. tried on some gloves. The gloves were those found at South Bundy Drive and at 360 North Rockingham. Nicole Brown Simpson had bought an identical pair for O.J. at Bloomingdale's department store in New York City just before Christmas, 1990. There was a credit card receipt to prove it. If the gloves fit, it would be a victory for the prosecution. The gloves had gone through tests in the laboratories and were saturated with dangerous chemicals, so O.J. would have to wear latex gloves under the leather gloves to protect his hands. At the front of the courtroom Simpson pulled on the protective latex gloves, then tried to pull the leather gloves over them. The jury and millions watching on television saw clearly that the gloves did not fit.

The prosecution thought the incident with the gloves was about as bad as the case could get. They were wrong. There

Judge Lance Ito shouting at defense attorney Barry Scheck during the Simpson trial. (AP/Wide World Photos)

was more to come. Mark Fuhrman's racist remarks now became the central issue in the trial. Years before the murders took place, a writer working on a television script about the LAPD met Fuhrman and taped several conversations with him. When Simpson's defense team asked for the tapes, she turned them over. The defense pressed Judge Ito to allow the tapes to be released. They included Mark Fuhrman's voice clearly saying, "You do what you're told, understand, nigger?" and, "These niggers, they run like rabbits." There was more, much more, but the defense had made its point. Fuhrman had lied when he told the court he had not, in the last ten years, used the word "nigger." Many now believed that Fuhrman was capable of trying to frame O.J. Simpson.

Marcia Clark tried to save the situation in her summation at the end of the trial. Did Mark Fuhrman lie to the jury. Yes, she admitted, he had. "Is he a racist?" she continued. "Yes. Is he the worst the LAPD has to offer? Yes. . . . Should the LAPD have ever hired him? No. . . . But the fact that Mark Fuhrman is a racist and lied about it on the witness stand does not mean that we haven't proven the defendant guilty beyond a reasonable doubt."

Clark continued. The defense had suggested Fuhrman had picked up the left-handed glove at the Bundy Drive crime scene and had transferred some of O.J.'s blood to it before planting it behind Kato Kaelin's apartment. But, Clark pointed out, the first officer at the crime scene had arrived hours before Fuhrman and had not seen a second glove.

She went on to lay out the prosecution's reconstruction of the crime. O.J. had gone to Nicole's house with the intention of murdering her. He was surprised by Goldman's appearance and ended up killing him, too. Then he hurried home to catch his plane to Chicago. He "ran back behind the house, that dark narrow south pathway . . . thinking he could get rid of the glove, the knife, in that dirt area in the back . . . and in his haste he ran into that air conditioner. . . . And that caused him to fall against the wall, making the wall of Kato's room shake. . . . Simple common sense tells you that the thumping, the glove, and the defendant's appearance on the driveway almost immediately thereafter are all part of one set of events, all connected in time and space. It would be a tragedy," Clark concluded, "if, with such overwhelming evidence, ladies and gentlemen, as we have presented to you, you found the defendant not guilty."

Cochran closed for the defense. The timetable set out by the prosecution did not jibe with the facts of the case, he said. If the murders were committed at 10:15, as Marcia Clark had claimed, O.J. did not do them. The results of the blood tests the prosecution presented were totally unreliable. As for the glove, "If it doesn't fit, you must acquit," he said.

The real issue, though, was the actions of the LAPD. "A good efficient, competent, noncorrupt police department will carefully set about the business of investigating homicides. They won't rush to judgment. They won't be bound by an obsession to win at all costs. They will set about trying to apprehend the killer or killers and trying to protect the innocent from suspicion. . . . Your verdict in this case . . .

talks about justice in America and it talks about the police and whether they're above the law."

As for Mark Fuhrman, he was a "lying, perjuring, genocidal racist," Cochran told the jury. When the police "take the law into their own hands, they become worse than the people who break the law, because they are the protectors of the law. Who then polices the police? *You* police the police," he instructed the jurors. "You police them by your verdict. You are the ones to send the message."

Late on the afternoon of September 29, 1995, Judge Ito gave instructions to the jury. They must find, beyond a reasonable doubt, that the prosecution had proven O.J. Simpson guilty, he told them. In such complicated cases, jurors often take weeks to come to a conclusion. The jury in the O.J. Simpson case was back in the courtroom after deliberating less than four hours.

As the jurors prepared to announce their verdict on Tuesday, October 3, 1995, millions of Americans stopped what they were doing to watch and listen. The trial, via television, had become part of their lives. They had learned about Marcia Clark's personal life, her divorce, her two boys, and her feud with her parents. They had seen a videotape of Ron Goldman and his father performing at a bar mitzvah. They had heard the sound of Nicole Simpson's terrified voice. Their hearts had ached for the Simpson children and they had been revolted when they heard Fuhrman's vile comments. The verdict, they knew, would tell them something about their nation. It would tell them something about their system of justice, and something about race relations in America. It had been a long trial, too long, and they were ready to know the outcome.

Judge Ito asked O.J. Simpson to rise and face the jury as the clerk read the verdict. "We the jury," she read, "find the defendant, Orenthal James Simpson, not guilty of the crime of murder . . . a felony, upon Nicole Brown Simpson, a human being." She continued. Simpson was also "not guilty" of the murder of Ronald Lyle Goldman, "a human being."

O.J. Simpson would go free. In offices, on streets, in restaurants, and homes, the nation erupted in response. Black and white America reacted in different ways. At a shelter for battered women, African-American women cheered. At Howard University law school, a historically black institution in Washington, D.C., students burst into shouts of triumph. Many whites were stunned. TV talk show hosts continued their obsession with the trial, spending countless hours analyzing the reactions.

The American judicial system offers more than one road in the search for truth. After the criminal trial, the families of Ronald Goldman and Nicole Brown Simpson sought a civil trial. Fred Goldman had followed the criminal trial closely, talking with reporters after each day's proceedings. He expressed his emotions openly in court, and cried when the verdict was announced. Goldman spearheaded a campaign to raise money and support for a civil trial.

In a civil trial the plaintiff must only prove the defendant guilty with a "preponderance of evidence." It is a far less demanding task than the "beyond a reasonable doubt" requirements of a criminal case. The Goldmans and Browns filed a civil suit charging O.J. Simpson with the wrongful deaths of the murder victims and seeking monetary awards.

At the trial, held in suburban Los Angeles, Judge Hiroshi Fujisaki limited much of the evidence admitted in the criminal trial. The Fuhrman tapes were ruled inadmissible. So were testimonies inferring that the police had planted evidence. And no television cameras were allowed in the courtroom. Furthermore, sources now came forward with a photograph of O.J. Simpson wearing a pair of Bruno Magli shoes, shoes he had earlier denied ever owning. In a speedy trial, the all-white jury found Simpson guilty of both the

O.J. Simpson, with attorneys F. Lee Bailey (left) and Johnnie Cochran, Jr., hears the jury's "not guilty" verdict. (AP/Wide World Photos)

murders of Ron Goldman and Nicole Brown Simpson. O.J. Simpson was ordered to pay each family $12.5 million. It would not bring back their children and siblings, but it might, they hoped, strip Simpson of his considerable wealth.

The interest in the Simpson trial refused to die, even after the decision in the civil trial. Marcia Clark wrote a book about the criminal trial. So, too, did Johnnie Cochran, Chris Darden, and Mark Fuhrman. O.J. Simpson's girlfriend wrote her account of the story, as did a woman friend of Nicole Brown Simpson's. The obsession with the case lessened as time went on but it did not disappear.

It has been, many thought, the trial to end all trials. But soon new cases were crowding the courts, cases involving new plaintiffs, new defendants, new attorneys, new judges, and new issues. The search for justice continued as Americans watched and listened with fascination, ready for the next sensational trial.

BIBLIOGRAPHY

THE SACCO-VANZETTI TRIAL

EHRMANN, HERBERT B. *The Case that Will Not Die: Commonwealth vs. Sacco and Vanzetti.* Boston: Little, Brown and Company, 1969.

JACKSON, BRIAN. *The Black Flag: A Look Back at the Strange Case of Nicola Sacco and Bartolomeo Vanzetti.* Boston, London and Henley-on-Thames: Routledge & Kegan Paul Ltd, 1981.

The Sacco-Vanzetti Case: Transcript of the Record of the Trial of Nicola Sacco and Bartolomeo Vanzetti in the Courts of Massachusetts and Subsequent Proceedings 1920-7. Volumes I-VI. Mamoroneck, NY: Paul P. Appel, Publishers, 1969.

THE SCOPES "MONKEY TRIAL"

GINGER, RAY. *Six Days or Forever?: Tennessee v. John Thomas Scopes.* New York: Oxford University Press, 1974.

LARSON, EDWARD J. *Summer for the Gods: The Scopes Trial and America's Continuing Debate over Science and Religion.* New York: Basic Books, 1997.

SETTLE, MARY LEE. *The Scopes Trial: The State of Tennessee v. John Thomas Scopes.* New York: Franklin Watts, Inc., 1972.

MCLYNN, FRANK. *Famous Trials: Cases that Made History.* Pleasantville, NY: The Reader's Digest Association, Inc., 1995.

THE LINDBERGH BABY KIDNAPPING TRIAL

FISHER, JIM. *The Lindbergh Case.* New Brunswick, New Jersey: Rutgers University Press, 1987.

GUSTAFSON, ANITA. *Guilty or Innocent?* New York: Holt, Rinehart and Winston, 1985.

MILTON, JOYCE. *Loss of Eden: A Biography of Charles and Anne Morrow Lindbergh.* New York: HarperCollins Publishers, 1993.

WALLER, GEORGE. *Kidnap: The Story of the Lindbergh Case.* New York: The Dial Press, 1961.

THE JULIUS AND ETHEL ROSENBERG SPY TRIAL

NIZER, LOUIS. *The Implosion Conspiracy.* Garden City, NY: Doubleday, 1973.

RADOSH, RONALD AND JOYCE MILTON. *The Rosenberg File: A Search for the Truth.* New York: Holt, Rinehart and Winston, 1983.

RADOSH, RONALD. "The Vernona Files." *The New Republic,* August 7, 1995.

The Rosenberg File: Case Closed. Videotape. Produced by The Discovery Channel.

BROWN V. BOARD OF EDUCATION OF TOPEKA

KLUGER, RICHARD. *Simple Justice: The History of Brown v. Board of Education and Black America's Struggle for Equality.* New York: Alfred A. Knopf, 1976.

McLYNN, FRANK. *Famous Trials: Cases that Made History.* Pleasantville, New York. The Reader's Digest Association, Inc., 1995.

PATRICK, JOHN J. *The Young Oxford Companion to the Supreme Court of the United States.* New York: Oxford University Press, 1994.

WHITMAN, MARK, EDITOR. *Removing a Badge of Slavery: The Record of Brown v. Board of Education.* Princeton and New York: Markus Wiener Publishing, Inc., 1993.

THE WATERGATE TRIALS

BERNSTEIN, CARL AND BOB WOODWARD *All the President's Men.* New York: Simon & Schuster, 1974.

JAWORSKI, LEON. *The Right and the Power: The Prosecution of Watergate.* New York: Reader's Digest Press. Distributed by Thomas Y. Crowell Company, 1976.

SIRICA, JOHN J. *To Set the Record Straight: The Break-in, the Tapes, the Conspirators, the Pardon.* New York: Norton, 1979.

Watergate. Videotape. Produced by The Discovery Channel.

Watergate Cover-up Trial Manuscript. Microfiche. Glen Rock, New Jersey: Microfilming Corporation of America, 1975.

THE JOHN HINCKLEY JR., TRIAL

CAPLAN, LINCOLN. *The Insanity Defense and the Trial of John W. Hinckley, Jr.* Boston:

D. R. Godine, 1984.

CLARKE, JAMES. *On Being Mad or Merely Angry: John Hinckley, Jr. and Other Dangerous People.* Princeton, New Jersey: Princeton University Press, 1990.

GUSTAFSON, ANITA. *Guilty or Innocent?* New York: Holt, Rinehart and Winston, 1985.

LOW, PETER W., JOHN CALVIN JEFFRIES, JR., AND RICHARD J. BONNIE. *The Trial of John W. Hinckley, Jr.: A Case Study in the Insanity Defense.* Mineola, New York: The Foundation Press, Inc., 1986.

THE O.J. SIMPSON CASE

ABRAMSON, JEFFREY, EDITOR. *Postmortem: The O.J. Simpson Case: Justice Confronts Race, Domestic Violence, Lawyers, Money, and the Media.* New York: HarperCollins Publishers, Inc., 1996.

CLARK, MARCIA WITH CARPENTER, TERESA. *Without A Doubt.* New York: Viking Press, 1996.

COCHRAN, JR., JOHNNIE L. WITH TIM RUTTEN. *Journey to Justice.* New York: Ballantine Books, 1996.

TOOBIN, JEFFREY. *The Run of His Life: The People v. O.J. Simpson.* New York: Simon and Schuster, 1996.

INDEX